ANTONIA CHITTY

Northamptonshire Libraries & Information Services NC	
Askews & Holts	

Designed and typeset by Greensand Design

Cover photos courtesy of www.istockphoto.com

Cover design by Greensand Design

Second edition published in Great Britain 2011 by Bookshaker www.bookshaker.com

Printed and bound by Lightning Source UK Ltd

All Rights Reserved. © Antonia Chitty 2010, The right of Antonia Chitty to be identified as author of this work has been asserted by her in accordance with the Copyright, Designs and Patents Act 1988. All rights reserved. No part of this publication may be reproduced, stored in a retrieval system, or transmitted in any form or by any means, electronic, mechanical, photocopying, recording, or otherwise without either the prior written permission of the Publishers or a licence permitting restricted copying in the United Kingdom issued by the Copyright Licensing Agency Ltd, 90 Tottenham Court Road, London W1P 0LP. This book may not be lent, resold, hired out or otherwise disposed of by way of trade in any form of binding or cover other than that in which it is published, without the prior consent of the Publishers.

Contents

Introduction   6

Chapter 1: Getting the Idea   8

Chapter 2: Resources to Get Your Business Going   16

Chapter 3: Business Planning and Organisation   26

Chapter 4: Business Finance   46

Chapter 5: Finding Customers   52

Chapter 6: Business on the Web   62

Chapter 7: Online Promotion and Attracting Customers   70

Chapter 8: More Ways to Find Customers   78

Chapter 9: Looking After Your Life   86

Chapter 10: Bigger Business: Taking it to the Next Level   96

What Next?   104

The Mumpreneur Guide's Secret Blog
As you've bought this book you can join me in The Mumpreneur Guide's Secret Blog where I'll be working through ideas in this book with you. You can also get extra expert advice and tips. Visit www.themumpreneurguide.co.uk/secretblog

Do you dream of a better life for you and the family? One where you are in control of the hours you work, and choose the work you do? If so, you're not alone. You're one of the many people for whom parenthood has been the spur to start your own business.

I believe that becoming a parent is a time when many mums and dads reassess their priorities. Going out to work every day becomes less important than spending time with your kids. And you begin to look for a different way to work.

Some parents are driven to set up their own business by difficult circumstances. If you are on your own with the kids it can seem impossible to find a job that allows you enough time to meet their needs. If work is hard to find you begin to look at different ways to generate an income. And if your dream of staying at home with the kids is slightly lonelier and less interesting than you thought, you may be looking for something more. Whatever your situation, a home business can be just the thing to allow you to earn, stay independent, yet be around when your family needs you.

I set up my first business when my daughter was just coming up to her first birthday. Spurred on by other businessmums on a forum I began to do some freelance work. I was over the moon when I began to make a decent living from my business, enough to justify my decision to step off the career ladder so I could be around for Daisy. I suffered from post-natal depression after that first pregnancy and building my own business was an enormous boost to my confidence.

Later, when I was pregnant with my son, I relished the flexibility to work when I could, but still take Daisy to and from playgroups and play dates. I had built up links with other mums in the same situation and used a range of freelancers and people working part-time to allow me to build up ACPR while remaining based at home. When I had Jay, three years ago, and again this year when I had my third child, Kit, I was so glad to be working for myself. OK, self-employment doesn't come with brilliant maternity pay, but the flexibility more than made up for that for me.

And I know that as my family grows I will continue to be able to earn my living while being there for school plays and sports days as well as illnesses and exam crises.

While this all sounds great, I don't want to deceive you that running your own business is easy. It is not. At first, you need to commit time that you could be spending with the family. You will need to invest in your business, and can find it takes far longer than you thought to draw an income from it. And you will face challenges and need to learn about many new subjects. Suddenly you will need to understand finance, sales, marketing and more. But it is well worth it when you get your first sale, when you meet your first targets, and when you are there for all the events in your child's life because you are your own boss.

And if you are worried about all the things you need to know to start a business, well, that's where this book comes in. It is based on my experience and the experiences of many of the inspiring businessmen and women I have worked with, all of whom juggle business and family.

If you wonder if you will have time to find out all the things you need to know to start a business, don't worry. I've done lots of the research for you. What is more, everything in this book is easy to read. It is written in short digestible chunks as I know it is hard to get time to sit down and read. And the book is packed with exercises which will lead you step by step closer to your dream business. While this book can't cover all of every topic for every business it does contain lots of pointers to help you in the right direction.

So, if you're teetering on the brink of starting a business, get stuck in. Start at Chapter One, and do your research on your business idea. Get help in creating the essential business plan, and find out how to reach customers and get them to buy. As you go through the book you can share the experiences of mums and dads who are running a business already. You will be inspired and reassured by what they share.

And, as a bonus for buying the book, you get access to *The Mumpreneur Guide's Secret Blog*. Every week I'll be sharing business tips and experiences. And I'll be happy to answer any questions you'd like to post. Just visit www.themumpreneurguide.co.uk/secretblog for advice focussed on YOUR business issues.

So, turn the page and get stuck in. Keep this book with you so you can read it and do the exercises at odd moments when you're waiting for the kids, or while the baby naps. It IS possible to build a successful business round the family. I love running my own business. I hope that this book helps you to start a business that allows you and your family to have a great life.

Acknowledgements

I'd like to thank my family who have become used to me typing away in every spare moment.

I'm perpetually grateful to Anita Angell, Kath Burke and Sarah Sadler all of whom contributed to giving me the push to get my first books published.

And I couldn't have started my own business OR written my books without the support of a fabulous group of mums. So my thanks go to Nadine, Sadie, Linda, Tipsey, Amy, Sarah, Bex, Vicki, Lou, Julie, Kim, Bonita, Erika, Karen, Laura, Lynne, Michaela, Miranda, Phil, Rachel, Sharon, Suzie and Wendy. You have all been generous with your time and advice, over and over again.

Finally my thanks go to Jess at Greensand Design for beautiful covers and layouts, Karen at Dorset Web Design for creating the site and putting up with my continual suggestions for improvements, and to Emma at Amberweb for editing out all the errors caused by writing this with a new baby in my arms.

Chapter 1 Getting the Idea

Do you want to be in control of your hours of work? Have the flexibility to be there to pick up the kids from school, stay home if they are sick, and go to every school event?

There are lots of opportunities to start a business which allow you to do this, and make a valuable contribution to the family income. Of course, it is not all plain sailing. Mum to two Laura has been running her own business for five years and says,

"It is still a juggle. I started off working every evening when my two were little: it got the business going but I realised I couldn't keep on like that. My partner got fed up too. Now, my daughter is at school, and I work when my son is in pre-school. The business pays for family holidays and treats. It is occasionally difficult when I have a big order to deal with and one of the kids is sick, but most of the time I wouldn't work any other way."

If you are unsure what sort of business would be right for you, read on for ideas and resources to help you get inspired.

If you're in work already

Before you set out on the path to becoming a successful mumpreneur, make sure you have checked out all your options. Building a successful business takes time and commitment, and may come with fewer benefits than paid employment.

If you already have a job, are you aware of your right to request flexible working? This may be the best solution for you and your employer. You have the right to ask to change the hours you work, and the employer has to listen to your request. You could ask to start and finish work earlier, or work fewer hours, or do more hours at some times of the year. The benefit to the employer is a less stressed out employee.

Do you love your hobby?

Why not turn your hobby into a business? This is not a way to get rich quick but plenty of women, and a few men, find that they can boost the family budget while doing something they enjoy. You may be an avid collector and want to turn your hand to selling as well as buying. If you are a crafty type, you could start selling your creations at local craft fairs or through online craft marketplaces like www.etsy.com.

Your rights to flexible work

Parents of children under 16 have the right to ask for flexible work. Make a written request to your boss. Once your employer receives your request he or she must arrange a meeting with you, to take place within 28 days. Within 14 days of the meeting the employer must respond in writing with a decision. If the decision is to reject the request you have a right of appeal. You must appeal within 14 days of the date of the decision. You have the right to be accompanied at meetings by a work colleague.

Your employer can refuse your application on a number of specified grounds:

- Burden of additional costs
- Detrimental effect on ability to meet customer demands
- Inability to reorganise work among existing staff
- Detrimental impact on quality
- Detrimental impact on performance
- Insufficiency of work during the periods the employee proposes to work
- Planned structural changes

Setting up a service

You may have a skill that will allow you to go freelance, like web design. If you have good secretarial skills, you could think about becoming a virtual assistant offering typing and admin services from home. Or, you could offer to do ironing, collect dry cleaning or wait in for deliveries for busy office workers. Think about what you could do that would fit into school hours, evenings or nap times.

Retraining

If you have small children, there are lots of initiatives to help you retrain for a new family friendly career. Ask your local Sure Start Children's Centre for information on courses with crèches. Call into the local college too. You will find opportunities that allow you to work with your child around, such as training to be a childminder. Or look at training in a complementary therapy: you could offer appointments at times to fit in with the kids. Alternatively, you might like to brush up on your computer skills and set up as a virtual assistant or web designer. Or join a creative course and start selling what you make at craft fairs on the weekend.

Look into direct selling

Direct selling involves selling to consumers away from a traditional fixed retail outlet like a shop. As examples, it covers door-to-door selling, personal demonstrations and party plan. There are many companies offering direct selling opportunities where you pay up to £200 for a starter kit, including sample products and promotional materials. If this interests you, pick a product you like, and which will sell well in your area. Check that there aren't lots of other local reps competing for the same sales. To be a successful rep you need to look beyond family and friends, and make the most of opportunities to sell at groups and get people to hold parties for you.

What makes a great business idea?

Find a niche

Whatever your business idea, try to find something that has a unique angle. You may have come up with an idea for a brilliant new product: there is more in the *Family Friendly Working* book about what to do if you have. However, most of us are not that lucky or creative. So, try to work out a way to make what you offer different to your competitors. I have already suggested that if you are looking at direct selling businesses, pick something that isn't offered by anyone else in your area. This same advice applies if you are setting up a local service. Try to find something that will make your business have a unique appeal. It could be the service you offer, the hours you open, or the people you are targeting. The internet has made it far easier to offer a specialist product and reach out to those who will be interested.

See www.familyfriendlyworking.co.uk for more ideas. The site also has links to lots of genuine work from home business opportunities and websites offering part-time employment, as well as an extract from the *Family Friendly Working* book.

You may also want to look at *Supermummy: The Ultimate Mumpreneur's Guide to Online Business Success* (Bookshaker). In it, coach Mel McGee has written all about finding 'The Big Idea'. She gives guidance on looking for a gap in the market, evaluating whether your idea can be profitable, and finding your 'hot' target audience. Mel says,

"It's important that you identify a need for your idea first before you invest time, money and energy getting it off the ground. You may think you have created an amazing product or service but if the demand isn't there you are making things much harder for yourself."

Here are three Mumpreneur Marketing Mistakes taken from the book *Supermummy: The Ultimate Mumpreneur's Guide to Online Business Success*:

Mistake 1: Deciding on a product or service first
Mistake 2: Kidding yourself that they need your product or service
Mistake 3: Thinking doing what you are passionate about is enough to make money.

I started off thinking I would write freelance features, and had already pitched some ideas and had them accepted. I saw a request for help writing a press release on a parenting website, and offered my help. Soon I found more mums in business asking for help, so ACPR started to grow. I now run the PR business and manage to write as well, which is ideal.

Antonia Chitty is author of The Mumpreneur Guide's Start Your Own Business book and runs ACPR, www.acpr.co.uk

I didn't really consider using disposable nappies for more than a nanosecond, and had bought my terry squares, when a friend of my late mother decided to treat me to some shaped nappies. However my daughter was pretty slim and they didn't really fit, and all the five brands in the UK at that time were marketing themselves as the best type of nappy so I got one of each to compare. I found myself talking at antenatal groups about the cost and waste saving issues, and on showing my samples of nappies people started asking where to get them and if I could help them, and Twinkle Twinkle started, about a week later – I had my first shipments on their way! I decided that online ordering was the way to go – this was 1999 when there weren't yet many online stores and certainly we were the first UK e-commerce enabled nappy shop to open. I researched and bought software (there were no open source shopping carts available at the time), designed a logo and the site, worked furiously over Christmas and opened the website for orders in January 2000.

Miranda Stamp of Twinkle Twinkle, www.twinkleontheweb.co.uk

I decided that online ordering was the way to go…
I researched and bought software, designed a logo and the site,
worked furiously over Christmas and opened the website
for orders in January 2000

I've always fancied setting something up from scratch and working completely for myself. I went on maternity leave from my old job with a very large company about 11 years ago and decided not to go back. I'd been doing direct sales for a couple of years from home and also helped to organise fundraising events for a local charity. I was tearing my hair out trying to find replacement stallholders at short notice for an event before Christmas 2007. I started to think there must be a way to make the whole organising of events and finding stallholders thing a bit easier – a bit like a dating agency for stallholders and event organisers. I was also very keen for it to be a useful free service for charities and fundraisers. I discussed it with my husband and Stallfinder went live just over three months later in March 2008.

Gail O'Brien of Stallfinder, www.stallfinder.com

I've always wanted to work for myself. While I was planning my wedding, I decided I wanted a guest book and even went as far as buying one of those white mulberry paper covered ones which David was not keen on at all as it looked a bit twee. Anyway, then I saw something about having Polaroid photos of your guests alongside their messages and just loved the idea. Thinking about it though, I couldn't work out how I'd get the photos into the book – would I leave a glue stick alongside which could be a bit messy, or what?

I kept looking online for a better solution, not knowing exactly what I was looking for, but on the off-chance that there would be something which would work better. I found Adesso Albums and ordered one (even though I'd already bought the mulberry one!) It cost me about £80 to ship over from the US as I couldn't find them in the UK. That started me thinking.

If I liked the idea then other people probably would too. I contacted Lesley Mattos, the inspiring lady behind Adesso Albums and pitched for the UK distribution rights. The night before I got married, Lesley agreed that I could go for it. I spent quite a lot of time on honeymoon worrying about whether I was doing the right thing. After all, I was working full-time in a job that required significant travelling, had a one year old son and a husband to keep happy. Did I really have the time and energy to try this? At the end of the day, I realised that if one of my friends was in the same position, I'd be encouraging them to go for it, so the decision was made. And now, almost three and a half years later, Instant Forever is doing really well and I'm enjoying it and my family and we're all a lot happier.

**Helen Blaber of Instant Forever,
www.instantforever.com**

The inspiration for my first product, the Baby Feed Wheel, came when visiting a friend and her new baby. He started crying, and she wondered if he was hungry, but couldn't remember when he'd last fed. I suggested to my friend that she use a parking disc to keep track of her son's feeding times. A few days later when I visited I gave her a disc I'd covered in blue paper, and the Baby Feed Wheel was born.

As a Mum myself I realised how useful the product would be, so kept going with it – researched, designed, applied for a patent and then had them made, and now I sell them. The first prototype was homemade but the finished product is professionally printed and hand decorated.

**Elizabeth Geldart of Chiggs,
www.chiggs.co.uk**

I spent quite a lot of time worrying about whether I was doing the right thing. Did I really have the time and energy to try this? At the end of the day, I realised that if one of my friends was in the same position, I'd be encouraging them to go for it, so the decision was made.

I was fed up of having to use toy cooking equipment for the kids when they wanted to help me cook. Their cooking accessories were mostly made up of playdoh equipment because I just couldn't find child-sized accessories. I was also very surprised at the number of people who don't cook with their children because they thought it was too messy or not practical – hence www.pinkfairycake.com was born. I wanted to create somewhere that mums could go to get child-sized accessories and things that would make cooking with children easy and fun. It is such a great activity to do with children.

**Jane Pope of Pink Fairy Cake,
www.pinkfairycake.com**

wanted to create somewhere that mums could

to get child-sized accessories and things that would

make cooking with children easy and fun

It all started a few years ago when I found a local cake decorating course. I really enjoyed the course and had a great time but I sometimes found it a bit daunting as I only wanted to learn the basics so that I could make fun cakes at home but many of the other course attendees were there to top up their skills for a business. I was often left behind or left feeling that what I had made wasn't good enough, even though it was quite good for a complete novice.

What the course did do for me though was to give me confidence in the kitchen. I started trying new things (funnily enough I've never had the time to do the things I learnt on my course) and decided to set up a business for busy mums like me. I've got three small children so don't have long to create perfect masterpieces. The idea behind Mums Who Bake is that most mums enjoy baking for their family and friends and there's nothing better than making a cake for your child's birthday and seeing their face when they realise that you really have made that tractor/castle/train/butterfly etc.

Mums Who Bake is designed to offer easy solutions to home baking and take away the fear factor. We have an online shop selling the basics, none of this scary sugarcraft equipment that you feel silly asking how to use. We have a forum to ask for help, a cake gallery for inspiration and we are also starting to roll out courses teaching the basics of cake decorating – geared at mums and not professionals.

**Vicki Hoskins of Mums Who Bake,
www.mumswhobake.co.uk**

Getting the Idea: Exercise

Getting an idea can be harder than you think... or maybe you have already struggled to find an idea that will fit in with your skills and your family. To make it easier, here are some questions to help you narrow down your options:

How much time do you want to spend working each week?

Which times of day can you work? (playgroup/school hours, nap times only, evenings, weekends).

Are you prepared to use childcare or is one of the aims of your own business that you don't have to?

How much can you invest to get your business started? (Think about costs of equipment, or whether you can use items you already have to get started. NB: Almost every business will need insurance.)

Are you prepared to take a course to retrain?

Now, turn over and have a look at some flexible and family friendly business ideas and see how they match up to your answers. There are lots of examples of mumpreneurs in business throughout the book, and some of their ideas may inspire you too. So, take a few hours over the next few days to look at these suggestions, and get some initial ideas for the type of business you would like to run.

Once you have an idea, sound out friends and family about your plans: ask them to sign a non-disclosure agreement to say that they agree to keep your idea secret if it is something no-one else has done before. Note down what you might need to get started: think about the resources you might require in the way of time, money and equipment. We will look at this in more detail in the next Chapter.

Family Friendly business ideas

	Can be done any time	Some flexibility	Fixed hours	Retraining required?	Less than a few hundred pounds to start up*
Antenatal teacher		x		x	x
Beauty therapist		x		x	x
Bookkeeper		x		x	x
Bricks and mortar shop			x		
Card making	x				x
Childminder		x		x	x
Cleaning		x			x
Coaching	x			x	x
Complementary therapy	x			x	x
Counsellor	x	x		x	x
CV writing	x				x
Decluttering		x			x
Dog walking/pet sitting		x			x
Doula		x		x	x
Gardening		x		?	x
Graphic design		x		?	x
Ironing	x				x
Marketing		x			x
Mystery shopping		x			x
Online store	x				x
Party plan/direct selling		x			x
Personal trainer		x		x	x
Photography		x		x	
Running a cafe			x		
Running a community mag-azine franchise	x				
Running kids classes – franchise		x			
Selling collectibles	x				x
Selling food		x			x
Selling handmade crafts and art	x				x
Teacher			x	x	x
Teaching assistant			x		x
Translation	x			x	x
Virtual PA		x		?	x

*includes insurance, assuming you own a computer

Several thousand pounds for start up	Notes
	Plus cost of retraining – may be funded by local NCT branch
	Plus cost of retraining if needed
	Plus cost of retraining if needed
x	
	Training costs usually covered by local authority, plus grant available towards start up equipment
	Plus cost of retraining if needed
	Plus cost of retraining if needed
	Plus cost of retraining if needed
	Plus cost of retraining if needed
	Plus cost of training if needed
	Plus cost of training if needed
	Costs can increase dramatically depending on whether you set up an online store yourself or get professional help.
	Plus cost of retraining if needed
	Plus cost of retraining if needed
x	
x	
x	
x	Depends on whether you own any collectibles to get you started
x	More investment needed if you need to make changes to your kitchen
	Plus cost of retraining if needed
	No formal qualifications needed, but most education authorities will ask you to take part in their training programme.
	Plus cost of retraining if needed
	Plus cost of retraining if needed

Chapter 2 Resources to Get Your Business Going

This part of *The Mumpreneur Guide's Start Your Own Business* book looks at the vital first steps to take when starting up your business. Get it right early on and you will find it easier to succeed, as well as saving yourself time and trouble.

Here is my top advice for getting started, based on my work with hundreds of successful mumpreneurs. You need to start your business by planning how it will all work. Follow these tips and links to help you get your plans off to a flying start.

Support

Get some support. No one can do it alone, and you aren't the only person in this position. Join a women's networking forum like giantpotential.ning.com, or one especially for mums, like www.mumsclub.co.uk or www.funkyangel.co.uk. You can also find support in the 'parents in business' section of a parenting forum like www.mumszone.co.uk or www.netmums.co.uk. If you are starting your own business, contact your local enterprise agency too. There are business advisers who can give you free advice and arrange for you to go on free business start up courses: find a link to help you find your local business adviser at www.prbasics.co.uk. Join an online business forum like www.UKBusinessforums.co.uk or www.A1businessforums.co.uk. Read the forum rules, check out the different sections and you will find an enormous number of other people running their own businesses and willing to share expertise.

Expenses of starting a business

Think about the resources you will need for your business: try to estimate what you will need over the next year, and take a broad view by looking at possible longer term expenses in the next five years. Allow a certain amount to get your business going: you may decide to spend a small amount on business stationery, eg business cards and headed paper, and a simple website and email address is an essential investment for most businesses. You will, of course, need access to a computer. Most businesses need a phone number: you could get a second line, or buy an additional number to point at your existing line so you don't have to give out your home phone number. You may also want to use a mobile specifically for your business, or even get a better phone which will allow you to receive and respond to emails when out of the office or on the move. This can be indispensible for juggling mumpreneurs who fit in work while waiting for the kids.

Equipment costs

Will your business need equipment? We have already mentioned the essential computer. Most homes already have one, and a home PC can make most jobs you need to do for your business quicker and more effective, for example you can use online software to set up market research surveys, and social networking to extend the reach of your business. If you are making or creating something or offering a service, you may need more equipment. Plan out the basics of what you will need, and guesstimate how often you will need to replace things. You will have to budget for replacements and upgrades in your business plan, and include an element for this in the cost of your product or service. Remember that you may need to move from using basic home equipment to something more robust: you could find your iron needs replacing more often, if you start to offer a home ironing service. As another example, industrial sewing machines can help you work far faster than domestic models.

Where will you work?

Most mumpreneurs start their business in the home, using the kitchen or dining table, or spare room. There can also be tax advantages if you set aside a room part of the time for business. If you are selling products, be aware that your stock will grow over time: most business owners aim to offer wider ranges to appeal to more people, and this can take its toll on your living space. Cost up storage shelving for the garage or spare room. Look at the cost of renting a unit in the local business centre: this can be less costly than a shop and may come with some services included. While your plans may be for working from home, it helps if you know an approximate cost if you do need more space. You may need a budget to upgrade your workspace. If you are catering from home, your kitchen will need to meet health and safety requirements. There are also requirements for your home if you are setting up as a childminder: you may be able to get a start up grant from your local authority towards this. If you are offering complementary therapies or beauty treatments from home, or even if you just want space to meet clients, you may need to redecorate one room. Some mumpreneurs remortgage to create an extension to house the business.

Boosting your business

Allow a small budget for advertising and promotion: we will look at this in more detail in Chapter Five. You may just want to start by running off flyers on your home printer, but you'll soon find it is cheaper to order in bulk from a printer. A small budget for promotional materials, and a little bit each year for a carefully planned advertising campaign can make your business grow. Factor this into your pricing from day one and you will avoid the dual dilemmas of no promotional budget or having to raise your prices to create one.

Starting with stock

If you are going to sell a product, you are likely to need money to invest in stock. Before you can spend, however, you will need to find suppliers which can take time. You can look at trade fairs, join directories of wholesalers online, search on the internet and even look through the telephone directory. You may find yourself checking the small print on labels of products you'd like to stock: finding great suppliers involves persistence and detective work and is an ongoing job. Once you have made initial contact with suppliers, you will find that they have specific terms and conditions: you will have to spend a certain amount upfront, this is called the minimum order value, and you are likely to have to pay for your first order in advance. Once you have built up some trust you may be able to get credit and improve the payment terms so you

Drop shipping

Drop shipping means that you generate orders and send them through to a supplier who delivers them directly to a customer. You do not need to invest in and hold stock, which can cut your start up costs. There are enterprises that offer to set you up in a drop shipping business, and some even offer to set you up with a website of your own. Some businesses use drop shipping as a way to deal with bulky or expensive items that they don't have space to store or funds to invest in. With drop shipping you will get a percentage of the sale price, usually less than if you had bought the stock wholesale. This can work well if you use it to complement other items which you do hold in stock, and can allow you to try selling new items at zero risk. However, if you go for the approach of only selling items from one drop shipper, and there are plenty of other people doing the same, it can be hard to find customers. You may also only earn a few pounds per item, so you can need to sell quite a lot of products to make a good income.

Find drop shippers at:

The Wholesaler UK: www.thewholesaler.co.uk
ATS Distribution:www.atsdistribution.co.uk

Puckator: www.puckator.co.uk
The Select: www.theselect.co.uk

have a few weeks to pay after the items have been delivered. Most businesses start off with small levels of stock. You will develop a feel for your best sellers over time, and be able to invest profits in building stocks of popular items. Alternatively, you could consider drop shipping, where your supplier holds the stock and delivers direct to your customer.

Time for the business, time for the family

Resources don't just involve money. Think about the time you need to start your enterprise. Most mumpreneurs will tell you how they invested every spare moment into getting their businesses going in the early years. The nice thing about this is that it gives you something to think about: even when you are cooking dinner or bathing the kids you can be planning your next business move, but the frustrating thing can be finding time to do it. If your children are not yet at school, look at how you can carve time out of the day. You will probably start by working in nap times, and using the evening or weekends to catch up. This can seem exhausting, but fortunately children get older, and more ways of making time for your business will arise. Anyone with children of any age can arrange play dates, so try to find another mum who would like some free time too and set up a regular childcare swap: you'll have her little one on Mondays and she takes your child on Wednesdays, for example. Once your child reaches two or three, look at local playgroups. A couple of child-free mornings a week can become indispensible. And every child can get some funding towards day care starting the term after their third birthday.

Other issues you should think about include whether you will need staff in the future, or whether you would like to work with a partner. There is guidance on setting up a company or

---

Buying wholesale

What it is

If you want to start a business selling products, you will need to buy goods from a supplier and sell them on at a profit.

Finding wholesalers

Finding good wholesalers is the first hurdle you will face. This can take time and effort. You may need to go beyond Google searches, and sign up for directories, plough through the Yellow Pages, etc. Talk to your business adviser to see if they have any tips, and ask around, although you will find competitors are unlikely to share where they obtain their goods from! If you see a product you'd like to supply, check whether there are any supplier details on the packaging: a bit of detective work can get you a long way.

Terms and conditions

Most suppliers will have terms and conditions about supplying goods. Most will have minimum orders – so you have to place an order over a certain value. This will vary depending on the value of the products but you could be looking at several hundred pounds. There will be rules about payment too. For your first order you are likely to need to pay before receiving the goods. After you have placed and paid for a number of orders you may be able to ask to pay on account. This means that you can receive the goods before you have to pay for them. Payment will be due within a short period, varying between a couple of weeks and three months, depending on what the wholesaler allows – 30 days is one of the most common payment terms. This system gives you the chance to sell the goods before you have to pay out for them and will improve your cash flow. It makes it easier to increase the range of products that you offer too.

If you create or manufacture your own product, you can read more about becoming a wholesaler in Chapter Eight.

partnership in the *Family Friendly Working* book (available from www.familyfriendlyworking.co.uk). The book also has guidance on the vital issue of business insurance. Will you need public liability insurance, employers' insurance, insurance for your buildings or equipment or professional indemnity insurance? If you are working from home, check with your home insurance provider: they will want to know if you are operating a home business.

Before I started my business selling traditional children's toys with a modern twist, the resources I felt I needed to start my business were suppliers, stock, a website and equipment to enable me to attend fairs. In reality I needed much more than that and more time than I ever imagined.

I had sourced some great products and had a website designed but had very little technical knowledge so spent lots and lots of time learning how to upload products, maintain and understand my website. The site was launched at the end of January 2009 as I wanted to be able to spend a few months working on it because I knew as soon as my craft fairs and events started up time would be limited, especially as I was still working in a job share and have four children.

My husband often commented about the time I spent online but unfortunately as I had limited technical knowledge everything I did took twice as long. I would post questions on forums and have to wait for replies or have to spend time researching what I needed to do. Eventually the products were uploaded and sales were coming in slowly, but if I knew then what I know now I would have researched a lot more and given myself time to go on more courses offered by Business Link or NBV and hit the ground running.

Toniann Harwood of Knot Just Jigs,
www.knotjustjigs.co.uk

I fell into being a Virtual Assistant, completely by accident during the summer of 2008. Being on maternity leave meant that I was craving both mental stimulation and cash! Me, my trusted laptop and www.peopleperhour.com is where it all began. When I first started I had a simple Dell laptop and a printer. I worked from my dining room table, with both my boys running around my feet.

I didn't have much in the way of spare cash because I was on my last three months of unpaid maternity leave, so I struggled to get my business off the ground with nothing. I worked all hours I could, day and night, building up my reputation and relationships on networking sites.

I won a whole lot of Antonia's books from the Giant Potential website and her book 'A Guide to Promoting your Business' was and still is my bible!

As a result I landed my biggest client in November, now I have six regular clients and am almost ready to give up the day job! So if anyone is living proof that small businesses can make it from nothing, I am one of them.

Kelly Cairns of KC Virtual Solutions,
www.kellycairns.co.uk

Another big chunk of money was set aside for marketing. After all you can open the most fantastic shop on the internet but unless people know you are there no-one will buy from you.

Equipment: My main requirement was a computer. Access to the internet is a must to conduct research on competitors and market trends. As we are an internet-based company selling e-books for children, all of our marketing is also via the net using social media as a marketing forum.

All of the authors were sourced through the internet, illustrators were found via www.guru.com – a great resource for finding suppliers from across the world in all sorts of fields – and www.voices.com have voice-over artists that can professionally provide audio. My IT team (primarily based in India) were found through a Google search.

Money: The main investment for me has been in sourcing illustrators, building the website, and the technology to turn words and illustrations into interactive, page turning, animated, read along, story books. Another big chunk of money was set aside for marketing. After all you can open the most fantastic shop on the internet but unless people know you are there no-one will buy from you. We sourced the initial funding via a remortgage on our home. This meant that I did not have the cost of borrowing to factor into my cash flow analysis.

Time: With four boys in the house my business had to fit around family life. Being global from day one has been a challenge as just as our working day is ending other parts of the world come online. So some late nights ensued to catch up. But the beauty of having an international team and customer base is that things happen whilst you/the children are sleeping.

From concept to launch was ten months. Far longer than I had originally anticipated mainly due to technical problems and getting the quality just right.

Making money online: There are NO fast ways to make money online. It requires a fantastic product, hours and hours of marketing your product, and a big helping of patience. However when your site becomes known and customers return, if you have a digital product you have a limitless stock that can go on selling.

Jeanette McLeod of EBooks4Kidz Ltd,
www.wizz-e.com

I went from working 60 hours plus a week as an assistant manager of a late night bar to becoming a stay at home Mummy. I can't say at first I didn't enjoy it because I did, it was good to slow down for once (even though a new baby is a challenge in itself!) But after around four months I started to get the itch to do... well SOMETHING! I started to search the internet for home-based jobs, a task that was pretty hard to be honest. There are so many scams out there and it is hard to find the real ones! I saw so many quotes, "I earn £500 a day working from home!" but I've never met these people. Then a friend recommended Usborne Books at Home. She explained it would be my own business, working my own hours, based at home so I can look after my son but Usborne would be there to support and help throughout. So after a little research I took the plunge and did it! Some may say I cheated, paying a little bit of money for a starter kit. Having an organiser's website where we can find selling tools, ideas and support isn't setting up on your own I guess but to me it's just like a ready made business. You still have to put in the hard work, if you don't work you don't get the pay, you still have to sort out accounts, sales, networking etc... and it is my own business but the start up was made easy for me. If I had done this myself, it would have taken a lot longer to set up and a lot longer to start earning, especially since I have a young baby to look after too, but I don't feel like I deserve the success any less because my business was set up this way. In fact I would recommend it to others who want their own business but feel starting from scratch could be a daunting process.

Anne Evans, Independent Usborne Representative,
www.usborneonline.org/kidzbooks

I sourced a long-standing, well established, toy manufacturer who worked hard with my ideas and designs for several months to produce a breastfeeding doll set, which could incorporate all the features I had initially drawn up, whilst covering the criteria for safety. It's taken over two years to go from an idea, to a prototype, to a commercially produced product. Although I registered my company in December 2007, stock did not arrive until May 2008.

Initially I wanted a manufacturer based here in the UK. I wanted every possible factor of my initial designs and prototypes covered, if at all possible, including of course the crucial testing regulations and CE marks which were essential. So we searched long and hard to find the right company for the job. It was actually my husband who came across a company based in USA and Canada via the internet. Once we had run through some initial questions about my designs and plans, they had a design team work alongside me with sketches, materials, testing, and prototypes, before we moved onto a production run. They were great to work with, and my design team leader regularly kept me posted as to progress via email.

Binkley Custom Plush worked with my designs, and the production runs were finally produced by their long-established counterpart in China. They have regular checks for their workers, for conditions and standards so I chose them, although their costs were much higher than other companies I looked into. I wanted safety and quality, or nothing! You cannot cut corners, when producing a quality toy for children.

Pip Wheelwright of Boobie Buddies,
www.boobiebuddiesbfdolls.co.uk

Resources to Get Your Business Going: Exercise

Now you have a business idea, start thinking about what you will need to turn your idea into reality. Work through the following exercise to help you find out. You may want to fill this in in broad detail first, then come back to it once you have done some more research.

My business idea (summarise your business idea in a few lines).

Equipment needed for business	Already owned	Cost to buy	Cost to hire

Where will I work? Write down your plans.

Where will you store stock, if applicable?

Cost of workspace

Will you need to adapt your house, simply buy a desk or some more storage units or rent office space or a shop?

Item	Cost

Initial start up costs

Write down a nominal budget for getting your business started. I've made a few suggestions which may apply to your business.

Item	Cost
Website	
Promotional materials	
Business phone line	
Advertising	
Accounts software	

Stock

List the products you will need to stock to get started, different suppliers, minimum order values etc.

Item	Details

Staff costs/freelance help

If you plan to employ staff talk to the Inland Revenue about costs such as National Insurance and tax.

Item	Cost

Time – when will you work?

Take a look at your week and write down when you think you can fit work in. This will help you to be realistic from the start about how quickly you can develop your business.

	Mon	Tues	Wed	Thurs	Fri	Sat	Sun
Morning							
Afternoon							
Evening							
Total hours							

And finally, don't forget the kids. You should factor in whether you plan to use childcare and what it will cost. You may be able to get help towards the cost of childcare: check out www.direct.gov.uk for the latest advice on tax credits.

My childcare plans:	Cost per week/month
Nursery sessions	
Childminder	
Help from family/other mums	
Breakfast/after-school club	

Chapter 3 Business Planning and Organisation

In this part of
*The Mumpreneur
Guide's Start
Your Own
Business* book
you can find out
all about how to
create a business
plan, what it is
for, and how to
use it.

What is a business plan?

A business plan is a short, written document which contains information
about your business – what you want to achieve and how you are going to
go about it. It also contains details of your business's growth potential and
some financial information.

Why have a business plan?

If you need finance for your business, the bank or investor will ask you for a
business plan. This will need to have plenty of detail so you can convince
them that your business is worth investing in.

Most mumpreneurs start their business without major investment, so you
may be wondering why you need a business plan. Well, a plan can help
you grow your business in the way you want. Without a plan it is harder to
know if each activity you do is moving you towards your goals. Read on
about the different parts of the plan and you will find out more about how a
business plan can help you.

Even if you do not want to write up a formal plan, make notes as you go
along as it can help you expose weaknesses in your business idea and fill
out areas that you have not yet thought about.

And, if you have an existing business, this is still a worthwhile exercise.
It is easy to carry on without thinking about where the business is going:
taking time to review can help you focus your efforts.

What to include in a business plan

1   Executive summary
2   History and background
3   Your business offering
4   Market research
5   Marketing
6   Premises
7   Capital expenditure
8   Management and staff
9   Legal aspects
10   Finances
11   Emergency planning
12   If you are buying a business
13   Other information

What each section means

Using the suggestions above, make a list of contents which is appropriate
for your business. Have a short summary and list the names of the
business owners. Date the plan on the front page.

1 Executive summary

Write a brief outline of your plans for the business, what you aim to do and
how you will do it. Mention the product or services, business location, staff,
target sales for the next year, and finances needed.

If this plan is to help you get finances, state how much you need to borrow,
how much you are investing and where the money is coming from, such as
personal savings. At this point a summary of the business finances is

important if your business is already up and running. New businesses should just include a forecast for the next year or two. Add comments if you need to explain growth or diminished sales.

You may find it easiest to come back to this section when you have completed the remainder of the plan: remember that you are summarising the highlights and key points.

Your plans for the business, what you aim to do

Product / service:

_____

_____

_____

_____

_____

Business location:

_____

_____

_____

_____

Staff:

_____

_____

_____

_____

Target sales for the next year:

_____

_____

_____

_____

Finances

How much you need to borrow:

_____

_____

_____

How much you are investing:

_____

_____

_____

_____

Where your investment is coming from:

_____

_____

_____

A summary of the business finances (if your business is already up and running):

_____

_____

_____

A forecast for the next year or two:

_____

_____

_____

_____

2 History and background

Write about your training, qualifications and experience relevant to the business. Write about how your business started, or why you are starting it. Explain what is unique and why you are well placed to run the business. Mention if you are a new business or a franchise. List objectives so you can focus on what you want to achieve. Be as specific as possible, and make the examples measurable so you know whether you achieve them. Have short-term, medium-term and long-term objectives – up to twelve months, one to three years and up to five years. Spend time planning your objectives. Some may be more personal objectives than business objectives, but make sure that your business will help you meet your own goals too.

Make rough notes about what you might include in this section of the business plan:

_____

_____

Your training / qualifications:

_____

_____

_____

Your experience relevant to the business and why you are well placed to run the business:

_____

_____

_____

How and when your business started / why and when you are starting it:

_____

_____

_____

What is unique about the business:

_____

_____

_____

One of the most important things to get right is your aims and objectives. Think about the AIM for your business. This is a broad outline of what you want the business to do.

_____

_____

_____

_____

Then, look at breaking your aim down into objectives. An objective is a measurable step that will make progress towards your overall aim. You will probably need a handful of goals to work towards, with some short-term, some medium-term and some longer-term ones. It can help if your goals are SMART – **S**pecific, **M**easurable, **A**chievable, **R**ealistic and **T**ime-specific – ie set a time over which you'll achieve the goal. I've left space for around four goals for the short-, medium- and long-term. Don't feel that you have to have four in each time period: equally, feel free to add in further goals if relevant to you and your business.

Long-term Goals

Goal 1 _____

Goal 2 _____

Goal 3 _____

Goal 4 _____

Medium-term Goals

Goal 1 _____

Goal 2 _____

Goal 3 _____

Goal 4 _____

Short-term Goals

Goal 1 _____

Goal 2 _____

Goal 3 _____

Goal 4 _____

3 Your business offering

Describe what your business offers. How is it created, stored, delivered? What other similar items are already available? Who will buy it? What makes your offering different or better? Again, this is a vital area to get right, and can make your business succeed or fail. Know what makes your business different to any other, and you will be able to start to get your business noticed and create sales. Also mention how you will ensure a constant supply and maintain consistent high quality. Include details of suppliers and their terms of trading, discounts and credit.

Describe what your business offers:

_____

_____

_____

How is it created?

_____

_____

How is it stored?

_____

_____

How is it delivered?

_____

_____

What other similar items are already available?

_____

_____

Who will buy it?

_____

_____

How will you ensure a constant supply and maintain consistent high quality?

_____

_____

What makes your offering different or better?

_____

_____

Details of suppliers and their terms of trading, discounts and credit:

_____

_____

_____

_____

_____

4 Market research

Write about what you have done to show there is a market for your business. Depending on what sort of business you are planning, you may be able to look up trade journals and business reports to help you understand the state of the market. You can start by looking on the internet, but may get further in your local library or by asking for help at your local enterprise centre as some business sector reports require subscriptions.

Where will you look for information on your business sector?

_____

_____

_____

_____

_____

_____

_____

Who will you be selling to?

Explain the groups your business will provide services or products for. You may want to survey your potential market about their buying habits to provide facts about what they are looking for.

_____

_____

Who is your target market?

_____

_____

Use a service like www.surveymonkey.com to develop an online survey – but remember that some people are more likely to fill in a paper survey. Think about which method is most likely to reach your potential customers or whether you should use both printed and online surveys.

What sort of questions might you include in a market research survey? This could look at potential customers' spending habits, the need for your product or service, frequency of purchase etc. You might also take the opportunity to find out how to reach customers: ask them what they read/watch, where they go, and where they might look for information on your product or service.

_____

_____

_____

_____

Competition

Note down any competing businesses and explain how your business will compete with them:

_____

_____

_____

_____

_____

_____

_____

_____

Pricing

It is vital to work out the costs of providing your products or services so you know how much to charge. Show how you have worked out your prices. Tie this into results from surveying potential customers to show that your business offer matches their budget and expected spend.

_____

_____

_____

_____

_____

_____

_____

_____

SWOT analysis

Work out the **S**trengths and **W**eaknesses of your business, the **O**pportunities for your business and the potential **T**hreats. This will help you assess how your business is placed compared to competitors. You can also carry out a PEST analysis, looking at external factors: the **P**olitical, **E**conomic, **S**ocial, and **T**echnological environment and how it will affect your business.

It is worth getting to grips with thinking about this sort of analysis as it will help you show potential funders that you have thought about all sorts of issues which may affect your business. You can also add **L**egal and **E**nvironmental factors to your analysis:

Strengths _____

Weaknesses _____

Opportunities _____

Threats _____

Political _____

Economic _____

Social _____

Technological _____

Legal _____

Environmental _____

5 Marketing

How will you reach your target audience?

Firstly, be focused about who you are reaching out to – look at age, sex, location lifestyle, etc. If you have a new business idea, you may be guessing at the characteristics of your potential customer. If you have a business up and running, make sure you ask people about the following in your survey. Fill in the section below with what you know about your customers.

Your customer/potential customer's age range, eg most purchasers are between 25 and 45:

\
\

Your customer / potential customer's sex, eg 73% are female:

\
\

Your customer / potential customer's location, eg rural, suburban, urban, UK, overseas:

\
\

Are there any other relevant lifestyle factors, eg new parents, parents to teens, childless, single/married. Note down factors relevant to your potential customers:

\
\

Work out the costs of marketing too. Chapters Five and Eight look at promotion, so you may want to work through these and create an outline promotion plan before finalising costs and summarising your plans:

\
\
\
\

6 Premises

Think about whether you need premises. Working from home keeps your costs down and increases your flexibility. However, there is a limit to the size of business you can operate from home, and mumpreneurs who are aiming high should think about premises at some point.

Choose premises carefully. Look at location, accessibility, parking. How much space do you need? In the plan, write down details of the size, costs of setting up and improving the property with quotes from builders. Note down if you own the freehold or lease, and how long the lease is. What is the rent or mortgage payment each month? Get advice before committing to a lease.

Where are you working from?

Size:

_____

_____

Length of lease, freehold/leasehold:

_____

_____

Costs

Adaptation/building work:

_____

_____

_____

Rent/mortgage:

_____

_____

_____

Rates:

_____

_____

Insurance:

_____

_____

_____

7 Capital expenditure

As we mentioned in Chapter Two, you may need to invest in equipment for your business. This is called capital expenditure. Consider what equipment you have and what you will need to purchase? Will it be new or second hand and how much will it cost?

Lease or hire purchase can help spread your financial investment. Also include vehicles for business use, mileage, tax, insurance and servicing costs.

New office furniture:

_____

_____

_____

Storage:

_____

_____

_____

Other equipment:

_____

_____

_____

Vehicle costs:

_____

_____

_____

8 Management and staff

Give details of management experience and include CVs of key staff – this is essential to convince investors and banks. List the number of staff you will use, whether they are freelance or employed, their rates, hours worked, training, etc.

Your management experience:

_____

_____

_____

_____

_____

Other key staff: details and experience, freelance or employed, salary / rates, hours worked, training costs:

_____

_____

_____

_____

_____

9 Legal aspects

How will you set up your business?
- If you are working alone you are a Sole Trader or Proprietor.
- If you are working with someone else you may want to set up a Partnership.
- You may want to set up a Private Limited Company, which is owned by shareholders.

There are pros and cons to each arrangement:

Self-employment
- You receive all the income and profits from your business.
- You are responsible for debts if the business fails.
- You are taxed on the profits your business makes.
- You can claim your business expenses against your tax.

How to register
Call the Inland Revenue within three months of starting your business. If your income is low you can request to be exempt from National Insurance payments, but it is wise to make voluntary class two payments of just a few pounds each week, to retain your entitlement to benefits such as maternity allowance.

Partnerships

- This is a legal arrangement when you are working with another person.
- You are likely to still need to register as self-employed.
- You will have the same responsibilities and benefits as above.
- Profits are shared as you have agreed in the document forming the partnership.
- You need to be clear about who does what in a partnership

How to register

Get a solicitor to draw up an agreement outlining how the business is shared. A limited liability partnership means your personal assets are not at stake if the business fails. You have to register limited liability partnerships at Companies House.

Companies

- Running your business as a company protects your personal assets if the business fails.
- You are employed by the company.
- You are taxed through PAYE on your income.
- You will probably also have shares in the company and receive dividends on the profits.
- You will need an accountant and have to submit annual accounts to Companies House.
- A company can be sold more easily than if you are in business as a sole trader.

How to register

Get in touch with Companies House. There are many firms who will set up a company for you for a fee, in the region of a couple of hundred pounds. Some enterprise agencies can provide assistance too. A solicitor or accountant can help you decide on the right legal structure for your business. Include a copy of any legal papers at the end of this plan.

My business will operate as Sole Tradership / Partnership / Limited Company (delete as appropriate).

Other regulations

Find out if you need planning permission, trade licences or environmental health clearance. Ask your local authority for more information. Trading standards may be a good place to start.

10 Finances

Profit and loss forecast

This needs to include overheads, the cost of running your business, materials, equipment and depreciation.

Cash flow forecast

The cash flow forecast shows money coming into and leaving the business each month. This is an important part of planning and highlights where you will have bills coming in, so you can make sure you have enough money to pay them.

Sales and other forecasts

You need to create estimates of how much your business will sell, based on your market research. Other forecasts include rent, rates and salaries.

Break-even analysis

Work out how many sales you need to be successful. This is known as break-even, where your business is making neither a profit nor a loss. See the next chapter for more details and examples.

Basic budget

In the early stages what you can take from the business may be limited. Draw up a basic budget for food and bills, then work out the minimum you can live on.

Managing your finances

Stay on top of your finances, so you can monitor cash flow and prevent problems. Fill in your accounts as you go along. If anything is unclear ask a bookkeeper or accountant to explain. Simple computer packages can help too. See Chapter Four for more on finance.

11 Emergency planning

A business plan keeps your risks to a minimum, but emergencies still happen. Have you got insurance? What is your financial safety net if clients take a long time to pay up? And what are your plans if you or key staff are ill for a prolonged time? You may also want to plan for occasions when your childcare falls through or you have a sick child. Write in your emergency plans here:

_____

_____

_____

12 If you are buying a business

Your plan will need more information on the worth of the business if you are buying an existing business. You will also need details of exactly what you're buying. Get help from a solicitor and accountant unless you are a financial whizz.

13 Other information

You might want to also include your CV and that of all the directors, plus advertising and promotional literature, letters or contracts from prospective clients, more financial information and references.

What else will you include in your business plan?

☐ Your CV
☐ Other CVs
☐ Advertising and promotional literature
☐ Letters or contracts from prospective clients
☐ References

See Chapter Four for more on finance, and Chapter Five for more on promoting your business. When you have worked through these sections you may want to return to your business plan and add in more details.

Now you know the theory, make some time in the next few days to start working on your own business plan. It should be a working document, something you use regularly, rather than something set in stone which you never look at. If some of the sections here are irrelevant to you, and you do not need the plan to present to a financier, leave them out. If the business plan is for your personal use, add in the sections you will find personally helpful.

Writing my initial business plan for Mummy's Little Hamper, an online store offering unique gifts for mums, allowed me to collate all the ideas and plans I had been developing over many, many months and seeing it in writing gave my business idea structure and confirmed that I had a viable idea to develop.

The most difficult section was the cash flow forecast and initial financial estimates for year one. I was very conservative in my estimates but I found that it reduced my level of nerves when getting ready to launch.

Since launch my orders for the first three months have far exceeded my forecasts (due to some great radio coverage I received), and I refer to my cash flow forecast on a regular basis to ensure I am not overspending and keeping cash in the bank to pay all bills and not go overdrawn. I am now four months into trading and have found it very useful to go back to the plan, reviewing and amending it as even after just four months I have a greater business understanding and more ideas to make a more constructive business plan.

Jenny Rennocks of Mummy's Little Hamper,
www.mummyslittlehamper.co.uk

An idea plus a small amount of capital can be all it takes to start and run your own business. Last June, I came up with the idea for Bibble Dribble after searching the internet for affordable slogan baby clothes, for my little boy Ashton. I loved the clothes on the web but didn't want to pay the prices. So, I decided to research the art of vinyl printing and heat pressing and two months later, had two pieces of machinery sitting in my lounge ready to go. My plotter cutter, which is used to cut the lettering and logos, cost £750. We hire the heat press machine used to press the cut vinyl onto fabric at £50 a month. It has taken five - six months but we have now covered the cost of the machine we bought.

Then for a small fee I created my website and bought a few different coloured rolls of textile vinyl. I've lost count of the number of hours/days I spent creating my website but I was excited and determined to do it. After a few months my partner and I had come up with over 50 original slogans to go onto our baby bibs and t-shirts and that was it! We took photos of all the printed bibs and loaded them onto the site and within days received our first order. We've never looked back since.

Sarah Le Long of Bibble Dribble,
www.bibbledribble.co.uk

I run www.darlinganddarling.com which launched in April 2007. The idea for the website evolved from my family portrait photography business and having four small children of my own. The website is a collection of products and services all of which capture a memory in some way.

When the website had been running for a year I realised that it needed to have more of a focus. Writing a business plan helped me to quantify what my key objectives were for the business, this keeps me focused and stops me from wasting time on things that ultimately have no reflection on where I am trying to take the business. Finding the time and discipline to sit down and write the plan is hard when you have so many other things to do, however I firmly believe that the business is and will be more successful because of it.

**Coral Garlick of Darling and Darling,
www.darlinganddarling.com**

Putting pen to paper most definitely helped me focus my vision and establish the viability of what I wanted to do, which was to run start up seminars for mums in business. I felt that after writing a very basic plan, the next step to move the concept forward was for me to run a series of four pilot seminars to see what the response was from the entrepreneurial mums and the wider business community.

This was a massive part of my market research and resulted in valuable feedback that helped me establish a stronger business model, based on personal feedback and primary facts and figures.

If you are planning to run the business around the children you have to be realistic right from the start – everything takes so much longer to do and achieve! You could actually end up being a start up business for a couple of years! The growth of the business will also be dictated by the hours available to you as a result of the changing phases of childcare from pregnancy, the first year, pre-school and finally full-time school.

A crucial part of the Business Plan is actually planning the family calendar for the year and working out how you can reconcile the business and family commitments. By planning in advance you can prepare for the busy periods of the business. When planning the year for Mums in Biz I have to take into account school holidays, family commitments, my husband's travelling work commitments and extended childcare help before I can even begin to think about work!!

Plan as far in advance as you can! And try and have a plan B and plan C!

**Nicky Chisholm of Mums in Biz,
www.mumsinbiz.co.uk**

It is so hard when you start out to make realistic financial projections when frankly you know so little about kind of costs you will face and the potential returns you can make on them

We started our baby bath products business, Cuddledry Ltd, back in 2006 with a basic business plan. The crucial thing within that plan in the early stages was our appraisal of our target market. It is so hard when you start out to make realistic financial projections when frankly you know so little about the kind of costs you will face and the potential returns you can make on them – and although you still have to do it much of that side of things has to be guesswork to some extent. However, assessing your market is possible from the word go (and before!), so this element of the plan was critical. Writing the plan, from the market assessment onwards, is a brilliant exercise in working out what on earth you are planning with the business, and where you see it going. Of course these things evolve over time, often very quickly (ours was out of date totally within about a month as sales took off dramatically), but to set objectives and a clear understanding of your strategy and how you plan to implement it helps you to stay focussed and not get overexcited about things which change along the way which could steer you off course.

The most interesting thing for us from a business plan perspective was applying to go on the BBC Dragons Den programme. Our business was featured in October 2007 and we have become renowned as the people who turned the Dragons down! We received three offers of investment but took the decision to go it alone – we felt they wanted too large a slice of all that we had worked for. However – the application process was one of the most valuable things we have done as a business. It forces you to look at your business plan, marketing plan and financial projections with fresh eyes, and we spent about two months solid scrutinising every single aspect. We put ourselves through the mill and by the time we were finished we had a totally clear, fully justified and incredibly helpful new plan. Being pushed into addressing every detail of the business and questioning its purpose and value added more value to our business than anything else we have done. Our advice to other mumpreneurs would be to apply – even if you would never wish to actually be filmed – go through the process and stringently assess what you are doing and where your business is going. It will soon become clear what is viable and what needs to be dropped or changed.

Helen Wooldridge and Polly Marsh of Cuddledry Ltd,
www.cuddledry.com

In April 2004 my wife Susie and I formed a limited company called Plum Baby with the intention of taking on the baby-food giants of the supermarket aisles with a premium range of organic meals based on the principles of super-foods, despite neither of us having any background in retail or the food industry.

I was the commercial brains whilst Susie had the vision for the product and the recipes. After much blood, sweat and not a few tears, we launched in February 2006 and quickly became the darlings of the trade and the UK's largest independent baby-food company. Currently the business has a 6% market share, and retail sales last month will have exceeded £1.25m. When we raised our first £100k of investment from friends, we had a plan that suggested we only needed £400k in total. Within three years we'd raised close to £4m... How wrong could we have been! Lesson 1: NEVER underestimate how much it will take you to launch and grow your business. Juggling cash in a fast-growth business is stressful and draining of both time and energy. All the guides tell you to raise more than you think you need, and they're right. Once you've launched then the last thing you want to be doing is scrabbling around for more money, which can also be damaging for investor relations.

The business plan is the cornerstone of any business. Even if you are not seeking to raise funding from the outset, it forms a platform by which you can plan what you are seeking to achieve, and how to go about making it happen. It should capture your vision as well as what differentiates your business in your chosen market. It should identify your strengths, weaknesses, opportunities and threats (SWOT analysis) to ensure that you have performed a reality check of your trading environment. The plan should be a living document, constantly under review and updated each time circumstances change, for good or bad. I came across an archive folder on my PC recently and was staggered at the number of versions I'd created!

We started with a template that we downloaded off the web, and it was fine for starters, but after discussions with specialists in fund-raising we adopted a revised format which helped ensure that we'd addressed all the key elements that any potential investor would need to know. Subsequently we not only received many plaudits for the quality of the plan but we also were forced to keep addressing the fundamental questions that underpin any business: Who is in your target market?, how will you address them?, how will you make money from doing so? and what are your options if the plan doesn't run smoothly in the real world? Frankly, if you can't answer these questions you need to ask yourself why you're going into business at all!

Setting up a business is no small undertaking, and you need to be prepared for knockbacks from all quarters. Having a plan that clearly articulates WHY you are embarking on this crazy journey is a good way to keep you grounded and focussed on the objectives in hand.

Finally, no matter what the scale of business is that you are setting out to build, make sure that you and your fellow co-founders share the same vision and dream. A carefully thought through business plan is a great way to do this, as it provides the opportunity to define the business, the product, the ethos and values that you stand for as well as the intention to make a profit and – possibly – the intent to sell at some future point.

**Paddy Willis of Plum Baby and WFT Consulting,
www.wftconsulting.com**

When you work for yourself it's very easy to
lose momentum and to struggle to find that motivation…
Don't put too much pressure on yourself,
the SuperMummy tag is a myth,
you don't have to do it all so don't feel
that asking for help is a sign of weakness.

I launched a new lifestyle networking website for women – www.be-fabulous.co.uk – in January so my business and marketing plan was useful to help me keep focussed.

My top tip is to KEEP IT SIMPLE – unless you're looking for a major investment from a bank etc you don't need to write a novel for your business plan. One side of A4 is quite sufficient!

Ask yourself three questions:

1   Where are you now?
2   Where do you want to be?
3   How are you going to get there?

These form the basis of your business plan. Then set yourself some time objectives e.g. three to six months, 12 months, 18 months and split your answers to question number three above under these headings.

My other top tip is to KEEP BELIEVING IN YOURSELF, when you work for yourself it's very easy to lose momentum and to struggle to find that motivation, especially when you've a baby (my son has just turned one). Don't put too much pressure on yourself, the SuperMummy tag is a myth, you don't have to do it all so don't feel that asking for help is a sign of weakness. Find a group of women (like on be-fabulous.co.uk) who will support you!

And lastly, ENJOY what you're doing.

Karen Davies of Be-fabulous.co.uk,
www.be-fabulous.co.uk

Chapter 4 Business Finance

The financial side of business may seem like an unknown language to you at the start. Get a little help and you will soon get to grips with what you need to know to make your business a financial success.

Start by looking at your personal budget. Note down your essential outgoings. Once you are in control of your home budget it is easier to set financial goals for your business.

Personal Survival Budget

	Week	Month	Quarter	Year
Rent/Mortgage				
Council Tax				
Water Rates				
Gas/Electricity				
Telephone				
Insurance				
Life Assurance				
Groceries				
Clothing				
Travel and Car Expenses (inc Tax/MOT/Petrol)				
Holidays				
Membership Subscriptions				
TV/Other Licence Fees				
Newspapers and Magazines				
Child Care				
Children's Pocket Money				
Presents				
Credit Card Repayments				
National Insurance Class 2				
Contingencies				
Fun				
Other				
	£	£	£	£
Annual Total				£

Seeking advice

Next, get some advice about business finance. You can talk to an adviser at your local enterprise agency about planning your business finances. I would also recommend talking to the Inland Revenue, who have small business advisers ready to help you understand just how to use tax law in your own situation. You can claim many business expenses against tax, and the Inland Revenue adviser can help you understand what receipts to keep, how to keep good records and how to do your tax return.

Find the right bank account for you

Limited companies need a business bank account, and there are advantages even if you are going to be a sole trader. A business account adds to your credibility, and enables you to keep your money separate, making bookkeeping more straightforward. If you want a merchant account to allow you to process card payments you are likely to need a business bank account too.

Choose a business bank account based on a number of factors. What are their charges? You are often able to get 'free' business banking, but read the details carefully. If you run a newsagent business, for example, avoid banks with high charges for paying in cash. Look at any limitations on the number of transactions you can make fee-free each month. There are many low cost business bank accounts for start ups: check how long any special deal lasts for. Some of the best deals may come with online banking only. Have a chat to a business adviser at a local bank and see if their advice is likely to be useful to you. Do you think you will want to process electronic payments: some bank accounts will come with good deals for payment processing? And of course, look at the interest rate for the account too. You may want a current account and a deposit account too.

Creating financial records

One of the biggest pitfalls to avoid is letting your financial records get in a muddle. Start a simple accounting system from day one. It is up to you whether you write everything in a book, use an Excel spreadsheet or spend in the region of £1-200 on a purpose-built accounts programme for small businesses such as Sage

or Quickbooks. If you have a lot of stock and an online stock system, the investment in a system like Sage will save you time and money as you can integrate it with your shopping cart and update stock and accounts automatically. If you are offering a service and have a small handful of clients you may not need something so complex.

Bookkeepers and accountants

When I started my business I quickly realised that accounts weren't my strong point. I started off using Excel to keep track, and my virtual assistant created the invoices. Now, I use a bookkeeper to keep track. I collect all my receipts and bank statements each month, then hand them over to the bookkeeper. I create business invoices in Quickbooks, and the bookkeeper uses this programme to tie everything together each month into a record that is suitable for the tax man.

Depending on the size and scope of your business you may be able to stay on top of your own income and outgoings. If you simply note everything you spend on the business and all the income you earn in a way that you can add up monthly and annually, you will be doing enough to fill in a tax return. Specialist programmes like Quickbooks and Sage allow you to do quick analyses of where the money is coming from and going to, so you can stay in control of business finances more easily.

If you feel your finances are a muddle, a bookkeeper will take piles of paper, receipts, bills and invoices and make them into coherent records. A bookkeeper can also help with invoicing, VAT and payroll. They will charge £12-25 per hour.

An accountant can also help with your finances, and can complete your tax return at the end of the year. You will need an accountant if you have a limited company. Professional advice from an accountant or bookkeeper can save you money as they may be able to point out new areas where you could claim tax back on business expenditure. To keep their fees to a minimum keep good records yourself using a simple spreadsheet or accounts programme.

VAT

"VAT is a tax on consumer expenditure. It is collected on business transactions, imports and acquisitions" according to the Inland Revenue. You will be charged VAT on many of the items you buy for your business. You can opt to register for VAT so you can claim back the VAT you have paid. If your business income will be over a certain amount, £70,000 at time of writing, registration is compulsory. Once you are registered for VAT you must add it onto your prices. The standard rate of VAT is currently 20%. If you do not start off registered for VAT this can be an unpleasant price hike – or an unpleasant cut in profit margins if you soak it up yourself. Even if you do not meet the threshold for compulsory registration at the moment, you may need to register in the future so it makes good business sense to allow for VAT in your pricing from the start. If you register, you must keep a record of all VAT-rated goods and services you supply and receive. You have to fill in a quarterly VAT Return with details of your sales and purchases. If the VAT on your sales is more than the VAT on your purchases you pay the difference to the Inland Revenue. You claim VAT back if you have paid more VAT on purchases than you have made on sales.

It is worth noting that registering for VAT before you need to can be worthwhile if you have heavy start up expenses as you can claim the VAT back on your purchases.

Understand the terms

Profit and loss forecast

This needs to include overheads, the cost of running your business, materials, equipment and depreciation.

Cash flow forecast

The cash flow forecast shows money coming into and leaving the business each month. This is an important part of planning and highlights where you will have bills coming in, so you can make sure you have enough money to pay them.

Sales and other forecasts

You need to create estimates of how much your business will sell, based on your market research. Other forecasts include rent, rates and salaries etc.

Break-even analysis

Work out how many sales you need to be successful. This is known as break-even, where your business is making neither a profit nor a loss.

Basic budget

In the early stages what you can take from the business may be limited. Draw up a basic budget for food, bills, and work out the minimum you can live on.

Start-up finance

If you need finance to help you get started, there are a number of options open to you. The simplest way, and the way many mumpreneurs get going, is to make a personal loan to the business. This will work if you only need a small amount to get started. Note down your initial investment and the business can pay you back gradually as profits begin to come in. The advantage of this way of doing things is that you do not have to charge the business interest on the loan and can pay the loan back as and when you want. Additionally, you do not have to answer to anyone other than yourself about business decisions.

Some mumpreneurs borrow from other family members. This can give you a bigger cash injection if needed, but you may want to clarify exactly what the investment allows the investor to do. Do you really want your parents or grandmother advising you on how to run the business? They may feel they can do this if they have a financial stake.

Entering the realm of more conventional business finance, you may hope for a grant towards starting your business. Your local enterprise agency is the best source of information about grants as they are often allocated by area. If you live in a 'deprived' area you may have a better chance of a grant. You will need to have full business plans and fill in application forms. You may need to report to the organisation providing the grant on the progress of your business. The Prince's Trust (www.princes-trust.org.uk) is the biggest provider of startup grants, and if you are under 30 and unemployed you should start by contacting them. For the over 30s, there is no single provider of grants, and you should not count on this as a source of business finance. If you do qualify for a grant you may need to provide 'match funding' – the same amount of your own money as the grant to be invested into the business.

If you are thinking about a bank loan, most big banks are used to business owners approaching them for finance. In the early stages, banks may encourage you to take out a small personal loan or extend the mortgage on your house. This makes you personally responsible for the debt. If you have set up your business as a registered company, you may prefer to take out a business loan. This limits your liability if the business fails and cannot repay the debt. Banks offer business loans to companies, partnerships and sole traders. Banks will want to see a business plan with details of your projected finances, evidence of the funds you are investing in the project, and details of how the business will repay the loan. If your business is already established, include accounts from previous years' trading. Contracts with buyers to purchase your products or services in the future will also strengthen your case for a loan. You will need to supply in the region of 40 to 60 per cent of the start up capital required, and the bank will loan you the rest. Look at the advice you get from the bank too: you will want to get a loan from a bank that has an approachable business adviser as the bank will want to hear from you regularly about how the business is performing and whether it is meeting targets.

When working out the amount of loan you will need, remember to have money set aside as working capital, to cover costs until money starts coming in from customers. Remember to include the monthly costs of the loan, as well as rent, utilities, and insurance.

You may also get finance from a professional investor who will assess the likely success of your business and offer you money in return for a share of the enterprise. This sort of investor will be looking for a strong and growing business to give them a return on their money. Finally, if you are looking for investments of hundreds of thousands of pounds, look into venture capital. City investors finance a business, in return for a share in the company. This sort of investment will usually depend on your company meeting performance targets and financial goals. The investor may also want a seat on the board of directors.

Other things to think about

Plan your pricing carefully. If you plan to supply wholesale, calculate in margins so that your retailers can make a profit. They will want around 50 per cent profit after VAT, and you also need to cover your materials, time, marketing and distribution costs. Remember to check your payment terms carefully so your customers pay you in time for you to pay your suppliers.

Paying yourself

Perhaps most importantly, work out the income you need to generate from the business. It is unlikely that you will start getting the income you want from day one: even if you set up a straightforward service like ironing or dog walking you may need to do the work then get payment. Allow for a time lag for money to clear through the bank if you are paid by cheque or transfer. If you have a business selling products you may need to invest in more stock for the first few months or even longer, before you get to a stage where you can keep stock levels up and take money for yourself. Some tips on how to make the business pay as soon as possible will be provided later in this book.

Different business owners use different strategies for working out their level of pay. If you are a sole trader all profits are yours and you will be taxed accordingly. As a company director you can take a minimal salary then receive the rest of your payments as a dividend which can keep down your tax and National Insurance contributions in some circumstances: ask an accountant for advice.

Each year I create a detailed budget for the year incorporating everything down to the last detail. Each month I match the actuals up with it so that I can see how the business is performing, and so that I can know to the nearest thousand how much profit (or loss) I am going to make in that financial year.

Apart from the initial investment, publishing company Giraffe's growth has been funded by its own profitability. My best advice would be not to take on anything new without doing a comprehensive profit and loss on it, and to keep costs low.

Each year I create a detailed budget for the year (generated mainly through a historical cash flow) incorporating everything down to the last detail. Each month I match the actuals up with it so that I can see how the business is performing, and so that I can know to the nearest thousand how much profit (or loss) I am going to make in that financial year. It also stops me making impulse decisions or purchases and means that I have a target to work to, as if I was in sales – it really motivates me.

The only way to get through difficulties and challenges is by surrounding yourself with a trusted team or confidantes, who you know will offer sound advice and guidance. I have a top-notch senior management team who I can rely on 100% to do things or be delegated to and who I can consult on literally any aspect of the business. I also have a really strong, reliable and loyal legal team, accountant and distributor.

These people know what my vision is and are 100% committed to helping me achieve it. I am not scared of calling in those experts to deal with something, and paying for their time, because ultimately if I get something wrong, it costs the company money. I am finding that as people rise to their challenges around me, the less stress and work I have to put in to make it a success. Finally, any business owner MUST put a stake in the ground where they want to be. There is no point in even starting up unless you know where you want to end up, and the timescale in which you want that to happen. FOCUS!

Rachel Southwood of Giraffe Media,
www.giraffe-media.co.uk

Jodie Riddex worked in accounts for a few years before the birth of her daughter Caitlyn. Having taken a vocational accountancy qualification with the AAT, she opted to become a Member in Practice. This allowed her to take the plunge, set up on her own and she now runs her own accounting practice, Accounts by Jodie.

"When I started working for myself Caitlyn was only seven months old, so it was difficult trying to juggle work and my family life," explains Jodie. "Luckily for me, my family have been really supportive. My mum regularly looked after Caitlyn during the days before she was at school and during the holidays now. My sister has also helped out a lot with my workload and childcare when I have needed it."

"My top tip to any aspiring mumpreneurs out there would be to look out for discounts and special offers, especially when it comes to running your business. As an AAT Member in Practice, I have to prove that I'm up to date with current legislation. The AAT provide great quality seminars and workshops and by just entering one of their competitions, I can attend one event a year for free. Also, by booking a number of events in advance and sharing the places with other members, we have made keeping up to date a lot more affordable."

"Childcare can also be really costly. My advice is to cut costs by organising your time efficiently. For example, during school holidays I sometimes ask a friend to look after my daughter one day so that I can work to meet my deadlines. Then, when things quieten down a little, I'll look after their children and fit my work obligations around trips to the park or farmyard. This way I get the best of both worlds and still save money."

"My flexible mortgage has also been a godsend. Working in tax is a seasonal career. When you have to fork out to replace your IT equipment during a lean month, it's great to know that you can flex the mortgage payments and catch up again when things pick up. This way, I don't have to take out any expensive loans to tide me over."

Jodie hopes that her daughter will grow up to associate hard work with the ability to lead a comfortable and happy life. "Caitlyn is really understanding about the long hours I put in to meet my deadlines," says Jodie. "But a great bonus of working for myself is that I have the time to assist her teacher for a few hours a week, which wouldn't be possible in a regular 9 to 5 job. It's at times like this that it really feels like I made the right decision. All of the hard work and stress that went into building the business is starting to pay off."

Jodie Riddex of Accounts by Jodie,
www.accountsbyjodie.co.uk

Chapter 5 Finding Customers

Unfortunately, finding customers is where some businesses fail. You may have a great idea, but can you get people to buy? Make sure you do your research before launching. Ask a wide range of people about their buying habits to find out whether they might buy your product or service.

Whilst running a business selling something you have a passion for is a key to success you also need to check that people do want to buy your offering.

You don't have to be a natural salesperson to run a successful business. In this chapter of *The Mumpreneur Guide's Start Your Own Business* book I will show you some low cost and affordable techniques to spread the word about your business. As with many of the recommendations in the book, do a little promotion every day and you will find that the word soon spreads about your business and sales increase.

Creating your Business Brand

Before you start trying to find customers, think about the image your business puts across. Here are a few tips on ways to develop a strong brand image for your business that conveys the values that are true to what you are offering AND will appeal to customers.

If you are starting a new business, take time to look at other businesses that you think might appeal to your target market. Collect logos from these businesses. Ask yourself, 'What values do these other companies put across through their logos, adverts etc?'

_____

_____

_____

_____

_____

Gather other images which you think reflect values you want to put across for your business. You might be attracted to images of flowers if you want to portray a business that is 'fresh', for example. Look at your selection of images and write down the words that come to mind. Don't censor yourself: just jot down the first words that come to mind.

_____

_____

_____

_____

_____

_____

Circle one, two or three of those words which you'd like people to use when describing your business. Then, ask yourself which colours convey these values best. Hot colours like red and orange can portray a fast-moving business, while blues, greens and purples are more calming.

_____

_____

_____

_____

_____

Now you have some ideas for words, colours and images which describe your business. Think about where you will use any branding: does it have to fit on product packaging, head up a website or be used on promotional materials? If you have a good idea about where you'll need to use your branding you can note down the different versions which you might need.

_____

_____

_____

_____

_____

Finally, do you have a name for your business? I suggest that you go through the process of working on the values and image you want for your business before finalising a name as you will be far better placed to come up with a name that puts across the image you want to project to prospective customers.

_____

_____

_____

_____

_____

If you have several ideas for names, start trying them out on people who are like those you might want as customers. Remember, you may want them to sign a non-disclosure agreement if you are sharing confidential business plans.

At this point you may want to hand over a list of your ideas and requirements to a graphic designer to build into a brand image for you. Designers will usually create a range of options for you to choose from. Alternatively, you may want to start sketching out some ideas yourself, either by hand or using a graphic design programme. Again, test out your ideas on other people before finalising them. With your branding sorted, you are now ready to start promoting your business.

Planning

Planning how you will find customers is the first step. Spend a few hours with a big piece of paper or at your PC noting down all the ways you could reach a customer. Think about what your potential customers read, what they listen to, whether they go on the internet, etc. Spend some time in a big newsagents looking at the range of publications and working out which ones will appeal to your customers. Make a list of target media, and call the publications to ask for their media packs. The media pack will tell you more about who reads the publication, so you can see if their profile fits with your target audience. Find out if there are events where you could reach customers, or places where they are likely to hang out. Download the 'action plan' in the free downloads section of www.prbasics. co.uk if you are finding it hard to get started. Use a wall planner or diary to allocate a different promotional idea to each day, week, or month. You might decide to spend the first week of every month writing and sending a press release, and the second week on promoting your business online. You might spend week three doing local promotion – distributing leaflets to local cafés, for example, and week four on planning and researching events.

Set a budget

Decide on your budget for promoting your business. You may want to have some money for promotional materials, something to invest in your website, and something for advertising. Business promotion need not cost you loads, but if you incorporate a small amount for this into the price of your products it will make your life much easier.

Advertising

You may want to think about advertising. Again, look at the budget you have for the year, and work out where potential customers will see your advert. Look at your list of target media and the media pack rate card will tell you about the cost of advertising in each publication. Find out the deadline for adverts to be submitted to each issue. Don't blow your budget on a single advert: it may take more than one view for people to actually remember your business name and take action. Get some ideas for your advert drawn up, using a professional designer if you need to. If you wait until the last moment and call up you may be able to get some bargain advertising space. You should never have to pay the full 'rate card' price for an advert. Finally, don't be swayed by salespeople who call up and try to flog you advertising: unless they are on your list of target media, just say no.

Marketing

Marketing covers a range of ways of reaching potential customers. Think about catalogues, flyers, postcards, direct mail. Be careful how you plan your marketing. Think about your aim, first of all. What outcomes do you want to achieve with a leaflet, for example? What messages will it carry: how will it act as a call to action? What will make the leaflet stand out, what will make people retain it? How will you get it out to potential customers, and how will you know if they respond as a result? Think about swapping leaflets with complementary businesses as a low cost way of distributing your leaflets.

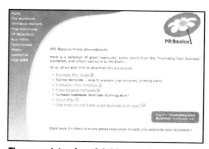

There are lots of useful things to download at www.prbasics.co.uk

TWO MINUTE TIP

If you are finding it hard to think of ways to reach customers, use your eyes. Look at what comes through your mailbox, study magazines and newspapers, and keep your eyes open next time you are in town. You will spot lots of ways that businesses are trying to get their message across.

There is also online marketing, a subject in itself. Having an attractive, easy to use, website, full of the terms people might use to search for your products or services is one of the best ways of marketing your business. You can then add in online advertising, email newsletters and spend time on search engine optimisation to maximise the traffic to your site. See the next part of the book for more on getting your business going online.

Press releases

Media coverage is a great boost to any business. Send out press releases on a regular basis, when you have something new to say about your business. Be careful to ensure that the news is well targeted: you can alienate potential allies in the press by bombarding them with irrelevant information. You can find a template press release in the free downloads section of www.prbasics.co.uk, to help you get started and write your first release.

Keeping your customers interested

The last thing I'd advise is to remember to keep your customers interested. It is much easier to sell to an existing customer than to find a new one. Use a newsletter or simply regular emails to your growing database of customers to share with them competitions, news, the latest products and exclusive discounts and keep them coming back.

Find out more

There are more tips on promoting your business at www.prbasics.co.uk, and you can sign up for the newsletter from my PR business, ACPR via the site too. You might want to check out my PR Blog, www.acpr.co.uk/pr-blog for regular advice on business promotion, or buy the companion book to this one, *A Guide to Promoting Your Business* which tells you everything you need to know about promoting your business on a budget and how to start planning.

Read on in the next chapter about setting your business up online and finding customers that way.

Finding Customers: Exercise

Now you have a business idea, start thinking about what you will need to turn your idea into reality. Work through the following exercise to help you find out. You may want to fill this in in broad detail first, then come back to it once you have done some more research.

What is your budget?
Fill in how much you have to spend on promoting your business in the next 12 months here. Note down any costs as you research different ways to promote your business.

Get some ideas together

Earlier in this chapter, I advised you to start planning your business promotion by noting down ideas about how to reach a customer. Here are a few to get you started, and space to write in your own ideas.

Printed promotional materials	Cost (if known)
Leaflets	
Postcards	
Catalogue	
Posters	
Business cards	

Look at Vistaprint (www.vistaprint.co.uk) for more ideas for promotional items which can be printed with your logo. Check out the resources list on www.prbasics.co.uk for printers so you can shop around and get the best deal on your promotional materials.

More ideas for promoting your business:

Publications my customers might read

Visit a big newsagents for inspiration and visit www.mediauk.com. Don't forget these publications are likely to have websites too. Contact the magazines to ask for their media pack which tells you how many people read the magazine and what they are like.

Websites my customers might visit

Websites will also have media packs with details of visitor stats and costs for advertising.

TV programmes my customers might watch

Think about how your products or services could feature here: would a local news programme reach potential customers, or could you enter a TV programme featuring some sort of business competition?

Events where I could reach customers

Find out who attends the event from the organisers – they should have details of numbers and demographics such as age, where they have come from etc.

Date of event (if known)	Cost (if known)

Other places where I could reach my customers with promotional materials:

Look at your list of magazines and websites, and note down four or five key places where you would like to advertise.

My advertising targets	Advertising costs (if known)

Think about the message you want to convey in your advertisements and literature.

TWO MINUTE TIP

Remember that it will take several exposures to your message before potential customers act. A single advert may generate little or no response, so look at whether you can afford a short series of ads. Always ask for a discount on the rate you are first quoted.

Checklist for adverts and promotional literature

What is the aim for the advert/promotional literature?

What do you want it to achieve?

Does your draft get across the key message and unique selling points of your business?

What action is it encouraging the reader to take?

Is it short and easy to read at a glance?

What image will reinforce your message?
Make sure the image is high resolution for print media.

Are you designing it yourself or getting a graphic designer to do it?
If using a designer, note down the cost for design

How will it be distributed?

What type of person will this reach?

How will you monitor results?

Now is the time to make a business promotion plan. You may opt for a diary or wall planner or do it all online. You can set up the plan in a way to suit you. I have outlined one possible layout overleaf, and there is a different one to download on www.prbasics.co.uk.

Activities to include in your plan:

- Sending press releases
- Sending newsletters
- Advertising
- Competitions
- Discounts and sales
- Local promotion
- Events
- Online promotion – see the following chapters too.

Example of plan:

April	Business promotion			
Week 1	Send out press release	Topic: New product		
Week 2	Newsletter	Topic 1: New product	Topic 2: Discount on slow selling line	Topic 3: Feature from complementary business
Week 3	Arrange advertising	Contact: Mother and Baby, Practical Parenting, Junior for best rates	Contact local NCT magazine about advertising	
Week 4	Local promotion	Go to cafés to restock leaflets	Research new outlets for leaflet	

I used my initial £100 on stock and materials for literature. Having created my own information leaflet I set about spreading the word locally to begin with. I gave talks at baby groups about my experiences and how the range of Amber teething products work which I am pleased to say were really successful. The sales from these groups gave me back my investment and importantly the impetus to carry on; I knew that there was definitely a market. I left information at baby and health food stores. Next I set about my website. Webeden offered me a free three months and an easy to use package to build my site with. Whenever my son was asleep or my husband home I was learning about and building my site. I also did all my own photography and editorial. Next was the marketing, I decided the most direct and cost effective way was to use the local NCT newsletters. I have been able to get editorial and adverts in various ones around the country which has been great. The Mumsclub network has been a real help as has their directory. I had a great boost last September when Ambersoothe was featured in the Mail on sunday. But mostly it has been recommendations that have made the difference. A product that works and customer service is the key I find. If someone wants to try something similar I would say that it takes a lot of effort and a willingness to have a go at anything. Never spend money you haven't got and you will find it very rewarding to know you did it all yourself.

Jess Blackmore of Ambersoothe,
www.ambersoothe.co.uk

Mum of four, Sabrina Pace-Humphreys, founded Trailblazer PR when she was 26 years old. Here she shares some of her tips on finding customers.

The main lesson I've learnt since setting up my business is that if you want new customers, the best thing you can do is get out there and meet them. In a service-led industry like PR, relationships are everything and you simply can't beat face-to-face contact. If you're passionate about what you do, your enthusiasm will win people over every time.

That doesn't necessarily mean joining every networking event that your region or industry sector has to offer. Whilst networking can be invaluable, it can also be a real drain on your most precious resource – time. Put careful consideration into which events you attend. It can be more beneficial to take an occasional proactive role, hosting a presentation for instance, than simply turning up at the same business breakfast meeting month after month.

Word-of-mouth referrals have always brought me a regular stream of business too. Maintaining professionalism and high standards with suppliers and associates, as well as customers, will encourage your own network of contacts to put leads your way.

However, when it comes to the crunch, don't just sit there waiting for customers to come to you. Never be afraid to pick up the phone and tout for business directly.

**Sabrina Pace-Humphreys of Trailblazer PR,
www.trailblazerpr.com**

The best advice I can give for anyone after coverage in a magazine, is to:

a) Find out the name of the person who deals with that section in the magazine (buy the magazine and look on the flannel panel!) and personalise your email.
b) Send an email that outlines clearly, succinctly and briefly what the purpose of the email is, why the magazine should feature it, and always provide contact information in a clear and click-on format.
c) Enclose two high res images with the initial email – this will avoid to'ing and fro'ing, which will always put the editor off. The images should be no larger than 1Mb each.
d) Follow the email up with a simple: 'I hope that you got my email and images and that you will use it in your next issue. Let me know if you need anything else.' Just to jog their memory. Don't be pushy or it will put them off.
e) Keep the tone light – light-hearted emails are always welcome but a formal email can be off-putting.

Most of all, you should be familiar with the publication you are targeting – this is where so many people fail in their PR.

**Rachel Southwood of Giraffe Media,
www.giraffe-media.co.uk**

Chapter 6 Business on the Web

Your website is the way that many people will first discover your business, so getting it right is vital. In this Chapter you can work through the essentials for any site and get advice on making it work well.

No business can afford to be without an online presence. If you want to run a bricks and mortar store, a website can work for you while your shop is closed. If you have a niche product (and I hope you do: developing a specialist niche is a sure fire way to give your business a good start) a website can help you reach potential customers who are interested in your specialism across the globe. You may simply want a brochure site to show off what you have to offer, but it is becoming increasingly simple and affordable to have your own online store and take secure payments over the net. What is more, writing a business blog on a regular basis is a great way to display your expertise in your niche area and build a following, while at the same time giving you a chance to add links into your website highlighting relevant products or services.

Setting up a website

Take a little time now to work out what you would like your website to do. Before you get stuck in to creating your own site, look at other sites you like. Make notes on what appeals to you about the layout and the functionality. Start thinking about the number of pages you want, whether you want customers to be able to buy online, the volume of products you are likely to be listing, and what will make it simple for you to pick and pack orders or link up your sales to your accounts software. You may want to sketch out how your site should look. And note down all the different pages you might need. As a starter, think about:

- Home page – to entice customers in and explain the benefits
- About the business
- Contact details
- A blog
- Product or service details
- Terms and conditions (see www.acpr.co.uk/terms.php for my Ts and Cs)
- Privacy policy (see my privacy policy at www.themumpreneurguide.co.uk privacy-policy.htm)
- A media page

I have included the essential website checklist from *A Guide to Promoting Your Business*, (available from www.prbasics.co.uk) opposite as I think this really helps you refine your ideas on website essentials.

Once you have a plan for the site, you need to think about some of the technicalities of creating it. If you know you want an online store, look at the list of store providers below. Some are very simple, and largely set up for you, while others allow you the maximum flexibility to customise them so your store is not a carbon copy of thousands of others. The option you choose to go for will depend on your technical ability and confidence. Have a browse through the different options and you will also be able to check out the pricing structures. For many of them you pay a small monthly fee. One or two, like OsCommerce and ZenCart, are 'open source', which means that the coding is free for you to use and customise. You might, however, prefer to pay a fee for something that comes with more support to help you with any technical difficulties.

Website essentials

Run through this list to help you plan your site content. Items marked * are required by law

Every site will need:

- [ ] Home page: a few lines explaining what you offer
- [ ] About the business: background information and further details

Terms and conditions including the following:

- [ ] A statement that the UK law is applicable*
- [ ] A statement explaining that the consumer is entering into a legally binding contract*
- [ ] Details of the ordering process and what it involves*
- [ ] To advise when in the order process the consumer commits to a purchase*
- [ ] Information about the availability, delivery and dispatch of goods*
- [ ] Information about substitutions in the event that goods or services are not available*
- [ ] Information about withdrawal/cancellation rights*
- [ ] The consumer's right to cancel – when buying online every customer can cancel as long as it is within 7 days of the goods being received*
- [ ] A clear complaints procedure
- [ ] Policy on returning goods

Privacy policy – whether you will sell or pass on personal details of your customers to other organisations including:

- [ ] A data protection statement*
- [ ] A privacy policy and information about security issues*
- [ ] A cookie (unique identifier) policy*
- [ ] An opt-in box for unsolicited email*

Contact page:

- [ ] Full company details – name, a UK geographic address*
- [ ] An email address*

Products/services page:

- [ ] A description of the goods or services being sold*
- [ ] Pricing information, inclusive of any delivery charges, taxes, etc*
- [ ] Information about how long the offer or price applies*

Other details:

- [ ] Any regulation or registration you or the business hold*
- [ ] Any applicable Code of Conduct*
- [ ] VAT number (if appropriate)

You may also want to include some or all of the following:

- [ ] News page
- [ ] Sizes, measurements of products
- [ ] Newsletter
- [ ] Awards
- [ ] Media coverage
- [ ] FAQs – frequently asked questions
- [ ] Testimonials
- [ ] Links
- [ ] Offers

If you want people to be able to buy your goods online you will also need:

- [ ] A shopping cart system. This allows customers to look at your products and services, select them and buy/pay through your site.

If you have a product which is available to other businesses, you might want pages for:

- [ ] Wholesale/trade terms
- [ ] Stockists

- [ ] And finally, you may want a program to count the number of visitors to your site, and analyse which pages they view, where they came from, etc. Examples include Statcounter and Google Analytics, or it may be provided as part of your web hosting package.

Ask around on business forums about how people have found different store providers, especially when they have had problems and needed help.

Online shopping carts

- Actinic – www.actinic.co.uk
- Big Cartel – www.bigcartel.com
- Cubecart – www.cubecart.com
- EKMPowerShop – www.ekmpowershop.com
- Moonfruit – www.moonfruit.co.uk
- Mr Site – www.mrsite.co.uk
- OsCommerce – www.oscommerce.com
- Romancart – www.romancart.com
- Store2go – www.store2go.net
- Vstore – www.vstore.ca
- WebEasyCommerce – www.webeasycommerce.com
- Zencart – www.zen-cart.com

Building a website

If you don't want a store, there are all sorts of software products and various websites that will help you set up what you need for your business. You can take simple blog creation software like Wordpress and use it to create incredibly attractive sites. You could opt for a Content Management System which will allow you to add and manage content for your website with the minimum of technical knowledge. Or, you might want to use something like Ning.com (http://giantpotential.ning.com) if you want to set up an online community.

You can also design your own site from scratch. You will need to pay for web hosting – virtual space for your site. You will also need to learn about HTML (hyper text markup language). This is the language websites are written in, and it is useful to understand the basics even if you are getting someone else to create your site. If you are doing it yourself, you can either create a site in HTML, or use a WYSIWYG (what you see is what you get) editor which shows you what the page will look like, rather than the code which is behind it, and makes it easier for beginners to create their own site. Check out free editor NVU, or buy a program like Dreamweaver. Once you have created a site, make sure you check whether it looks good in browsers like Firefox and Safari, as well as Internet Explorer.

> ### TWO MINUTE TIP
> When creating a website, most of the attention focuses on the design and layout. However, it is equally important to make sure you have quality content as well as quality design. So always remember, content is king!

Alternatively, you may want to talk to a web designer who can create a site for you. I've worked with a number of web designers who offer reasonable rates for mumpreneurs. If you are a net novice you may find it worth your while getting a quote from one of these businesses as it will help you get your business online more rapidly:

- Dorset Web Design
  www.dorsetwebdesign.net
  (created www.themumpreneurguide.co.uk)
- Glassraven Web Design
  www.glassraven.com
  (created www.prbasics.co.uk)
- Hands Up Web Design
  www.handsupwebdesign.co.uk
  (created www.familyfriendlyworking.co.uk)

Other web designers who understand the needs of mumpreneurs:

- Daffodil Design www.daffodil-design.com
- Ihelm Enterprises www.ihelm-enterprises.co.uk
- Jiwa Web Design www.jiwawebdesign.co.uk
- Naked Web Design www.nakedwebsite.co.uk
- Templedene Website Design
  www.templedene.net
- White Ochre Design www.whiteochre.co.uk

Going international

The benefit of having a website is that you can reach purchasers whether they are located in the Western Isles or the Isles of Scilly. It is important to check which countries are covered by your business insurance. It can significantly increase your premium to sell to the USA, so check this out and be clear in your terms and conditions where you will ship to.

Taking payments

Once you have your site in progress, you also need to check out ways of taking payment. Most online stores integrate with payment gateways like Paypal, Nochex and Protx. To start, Paypal is one of the simplest systems to set up. It charges a small percentage for each transaction and allows you to take online payments only. You can upgrade to Paypal Website Payments Pro which allows you to accept payment directly on your website or by phone, fax and mail too. You usually pay a monthly fee plus a percentage of the sale although there are discount offers from time to time. For a bigger business, you may want to set up a merchant account with your business bank using a secure online payment gateway like Worldpay, Protx or Streamline. This too will cost around £20 per month and allow online, phone, fax and postal transactions. Fees may include a certain number of transactions, after which there are further charges per transaction. Other schemes just charge you per transaction.

Business on the Web: Exercise

1 Research websites and start making notes on what you want.

What sort of site do you want?
- ☐ Brochure site
- ☐ Online store
- ☐ Blog

Which sites appeal to you? Note down four or five websites you like, and which you think might appeal to your potential customers.

Think about what you like about them – the layout, colours, ease of use etc. Write down the good points of each of the sites you have selected above.

What other sites are your target customers using? Ask people who could become customers for their recommendations and why they like them, and note these down here.

Now, use your research above to come up with some of the key elements for your site. This could be about the way it is laid out or essential features you want to include.

Take some time to go through the pages you want to include. Draw this out by hand on a piece of paper so you can see how someone might flow through the site. You should look at people entering on the front page, and also make sure that it is possible for people to find what they want if they come into the site via a different page.

Tick the pages you want to include from the list below, and add in your own ideas: ☐ Home page – to entice customers in and explain the benefits ☐ About the business ☐ Contact details ☐ A blog ☐ Product or service details ☐ Terms and conditions ☐ Privacy policy ☐ A media page	My own ideas:

2 Check out some of the web designers and software you might use to create your own site

☐ I want to design my own site
☐ I need to find a designer

Use the ideas from Point One to create a brief for what you need the site to do. This will help whether you are creating your own site or briefing a designer. Allow plenty of time to develop the site whether you are doing it yourself or need to feedback changes to the designer. Build in time for trialling the site too and getting other users to test it out.

My website timeline

Initial design	
Amendments to design	
Testing with small group of users	
Further amendments	

3 Think about how you want to take payments.
It can take some time to get a merchant account set up, and you are likely to need a business bank account first. Make a shortlist of companies which offer merchant accounts and compare their rates. Sign up for Paypal as it is useful to offer this as an option too.

Dadpreneur and professional footballer Michael Duberry shares tips for a successful web business from his own experiences:

1 Find a good name.
2 Buy a domain name with .com & .co.uk.
3 Design a good logo.
4 Search around for a good web designer.
5 Web designers don't have to cost the earth!!
6 Find a good bank that offers best new business rates.
7 Look for the best ways of advertising which suit you.
8 Don't listen to companies that say they can guarantee first page on Google as 99 times out of 100 they CAN'T!
9 Enjoy your business! Make it a pleasure never a chore!!
10 Make lots of money!!

Michael Duberry of Mummy's Online Baby Shop,
www.mummysonlinebabyshop.com

Don't listen to companies that say they
can guarantee 1st page on Google
as 99 times out of 100 they CAN'T!

beansprog.com is an online marketplace for children's items; new and second-hand, so we immediately faced the twin issues of tangibility and quality control because people are used to handling garments and can be wary of used goods. Because of this we realised it was particularly important to make beansprog a trustworthy and accessible brand; so user-friendly web design and targeted PR were key to achieving this goal. In addition, we helped to manage customer expectations by asking sellers to give accurate descriptions of their items.

Another challenge unique to the internet is one of payment exchange: with other online sales (and auction) sites the customer 'pays then prays' for delivery of their purchase. This motivated us to create 'the beanbank' which acts as custodian of the monies until an item has been received by the buyer.

A summary of the sales process 'flow':

1. Item is bought – beansprog receives payment (item price + P&P if applicable)
2. beansprog sends email (& text) to bringer "item sold, please dispatch"
3. Bringer sends item (or it is collected by buyer) and updates online account "item dispatched"
4. Buyer updates online account "item received"
5. beansprog credits bringer's bank account (item price less 10% beansprog commission) + P&P)
6. beansprog sends email (& text) to bringer "item received, account credited"

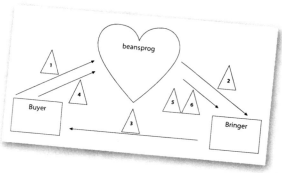

beansprog uses Protx as the Payment Service Provider, and Streamline as the Internet Merchant Account. Quite simply, the steps we had to go through to set this up were hard work and problem solving. If things ever got over-complicated, we always came back to our motto of "keep it simple". Overall, setting up a business on the web requires the main ingredients for building any sort of business: passion and commitment.

Abby Wood and Zoe Bywater of beansprog,
www.beansprog.com

Now you have come up with some thoughts on how you plan to set up your website you need to look in more depth at creating content that attracts and retains customers, plus the all important search engine optimisation.

Search engine optimisation

If you set up your web pages carefully, and include key terms that people will use to search for your products and services both in the page content and the hidden page descriptions, you are going to increase the chance of your page ranking well when people search online. If someone searches for a phrase related to your business, and your website is not displayed on the first page of results then your chances of getting visitors to your website are severely reduced.

Search engine optimisation (SEO) simply means developing a website that a search engine such as Google, can properly read and index. It is done so that your site will rank highly in the search engine results for certain phrases, as explained above. Part of SEO is connected to meta-tags (the hidden information embedded in the website code which provides information about the document and its content) but according to Sadie Knight of Glassraven Web Design (www.glassraven.com), it is just the "tip of the iceberg". Sadie goes on to explain, *"The main meta-tags in use are the <keyword> and <description> tags. Little emphasis is placed on the <keyword> tag nowadays, with only small search engines making any use of it. The best advice is to put your main keywords and phrases into this tag, keeping it brief and to the point, and avoid repeating the same word over and over again (limiting it to a maximum of five occurrences if it is necessary to repeat at all). Most importantly – do not include words that are not relevant to your website!"*

"The description tag provides the search engines with a short synopsis of your web page. A maximum of 250 characters will be displayed so again keep it brief and to the point. It has no effect on your search engine rankings and not all search engines will use it, but it is useful to include it for those search engines that will display it on the results page."

Beyond the meta-tags, you need to consider your page content. Optimising your pages is an ongoing occupation. Busy mumpreneurs put aside a few minutes each day to improve their product and image descriptions and stay on top of what search engines are looking for.

Keywords and phrases

The first thing that you need to decide is what keywords or key phrases you wish to target. These are the phrases that people will be able to use in the search engines in order to find your website easily. The more targeted the key phrase, the more likely you are to rank highly for it as there will be less competition. At the same time, fewer people will be searching for the phrases, though these people will be more likely to click through to your website as it will be more specific to what they are searching for. Again, Sadie Knight explains, *"For example, 'baby clothing' had 1,830,000 searches in July, and a Google.com search located around 6,870,000 web pages. In contrast 'organic baby clothes' had 1,300 searches, with the search on Google providing 477,000 web pages. (How did I work this out? I looked on the Google keyword tool which will tell you about the popularity of different search terms and also suggest alternatives.)"*

"Traffic to a website from the more specific key phrase will be more targeted and so the visitor is more likely to actually stay and browse the site. So choosing the right key phrases for your business is the most important factor in starting to optimise your website for the search engines.

"Different phrases can be used and targeted on different pages of the site, ideally one – three phrases per page – depending on the length of the page. This key phrase should then be included in the <title> tag of the page – which is the title that is displayed at the top of the screen that tells users what your page is about (and also the information that is bookmarked if someone adds the website to their favourites list). Ideally have a key phrase at the start of the title tag, as it gains most emphasis there."

Text and formatting

Use your phrases within your main website content – ideally they should be repeated around three times on the page. And keep the most important content at the top of the page. Search engines give most significance to the content found first. Make use of font formatting – BOLD text is given more significance than standard, so highlight those key phrases. Ensure that all information is displayed in text format. Images look nice to your viewers but a search engine cannot read them. The same is true of links – ensure that text-based links are used – if your navigation is image-based then ensure that there are also text links on the page in order for the search engines to be able to navigate your site. A site-map that lists all the pages in your website can be a useful tool for SEO.

Links and images

Ensure that all links are descriptive. If you were running a handmade wedding stationery business for example, to link to a page that is being optimised for the phrase 'handmade wedding stationery', do not simply say 'for more information on our wedding stationery range please click here'. The words 'click here' do not tell a search engine anything about the page it is about to visit. Highlight your phrases to link through to the page within your site, for example; 'we offer handmade wedding stationery for your big day'.

Where images or photos are used, ensure that a description of the image is used in the 'alt tag' (part of the HTML code attached to the image). Following on from the example above, a photo of a wedding invite could have an alt tag that simply said 'wedding invitation'. However, a more descriptive and useful way to write this would be 'wedding invitation from our range of handmade wedding stationery, designed to suit your colours and themes'. This way you can add one of your key phrases into the alt tag as well as describing the image in some more detail and giving the search engine more to go on. This is doubly important from the viewpoint of users with text only browsers, where the viewer will not see the image at all, or users who have images turned off as standard but can choose to view if they wish.

Become your own SEO expert

I'm not an SEO specialist, but there are plenty of people out there who are, and fortunately most of them blog and create articles to share their knowledge. SEO is a game with moving goalposts, so stay in touch by reading some of these useful sites:

- Check out the articles at www.glassraven.com
- Clickz www.clickz.com
- Search Engine Land www.searchengineland.com
- Search Engine Watch www.searchenginewatch.com
- Site Pro News www.sitepronews.com
- Web Pro News www.webpronews.com
- Visit www.kksmarts.com/lp/ how-do-you-web-optimise.asp to find out about using your keyword in your title and description tags and headings.

My current favourite site is Website Grader (http://website.grader.com). For SEO novices it takes a number of key indicators and rapidly assesses how your site is performing. You get a mark out of one hundred, can see where you need to improve things and what improvements to make. Don't limit yourself to what this one site suggests, though. There is a lot more to SEO than ticking boxes. It needs to be an ongoing activity.

More links to raise your rankings

Links into your site help with your site's rankings too. At time of writing, I have more than 15,000 links into www.familyfriendlyworking.co.uk, which I have achieved by making full use of all sorts of social media, and it makes a big difference. Some of the links are from external blogs, articles I have placed on other sites, link swaps… the list goes on. I rarely pass a day without pimping one of my sites somewhere.

You can also use other sites to raise your rankings.

- Recently Twitter has been the biggest source of referrals to my site.
- I've used Tweetlater to set up semi-automated posts about my sites daily and send messages about my sites to people who follow me.
- Create a video, embed it in your website and host it on You Tube, for example.
- Put pictures on Flickr with keywords linking to your site.
- Use sites such as Digg and Delicious to create links to your content.
- Submit your site to directories such as Aboutus, DMOZ, Yahoo and Zoominfo.
- Submit products to GoogleBase.
- Register on GoogleLocal if you have a business which needs local customers.
- Create 'lenses' – short articles explaining about a topic – on Squidoo.

Adwords

Search engines like Google and Yahoo make money by allowing paid adverts to appear alongside natural search results. The advertiser pays every time someone clicks on the ad. You can use online advertising to get your products seen next to top search results. This can help when you are starting out and don't feature highly on search engine results, and can allow you to get a new product seen right away. Generally, you set a budget for the day and a 'bid' per click: the higher you bid, the more likely your ad will appear. Your ad will appear until your daily budget has been used up by people clicking through to your site. Think carefully about the words you select to tie your ad to: for example if I choose 'Business', I'll need to pay quite a lot for each click as lots of other advertisers want their advert to appear when people search on the word 'business'. If, however, I choose a more specific phrase like 'business start up mums' I'll get better targeted visitors to my site, and won't have to bid as much.

Social networking

You can use Facebook (www.facebook.com/business/?pages) to set up a page for your business. This is another way to bring a different group of people into contact with your business. If your friends and customers become a fan of your page, their friends will see this too, and may visit your page. You can also promote news and events to people who are fans of your page, and Twitter is a site where you can write 140 character messages about you, your life and your business. It is a rapid way to build a network. Some people love it and find it totally addictive, others wonder about what useful information you can get in 140 characters. I can only say it is my current top referrer, and it would be daft not to use it to promote your business. Use one of the useful sites that allow you to pre-programme in some tweets, link it up to your blog so your followers know when you write about something, and include a mix of comment on your everyday life too.

MySpace offers a similar opportunity to reach new people. You can run a blog and send news and messages to your MySpace friends. Not quite social networking, but another useful place to be seen is BTTradespace.com. It offers you the chance to set up an online store for free with around five products: if you want to display more products there is a monthly fee. It acts as a good showcase for my business and my BTTradespace site http://prbasics.bttradespace.com, gets almost as many visitors as www.prbasics.co.uk.

There are more social networking sites: see Wikipedia (http://en.wikipedia.org/wiki/List_of social_networking_websites) for a current list. Try to focus on sites that are used by your target audience. If you offer advice on finding clothes to suit you, visit websites that focus on fashion. Post on fashion-based blogs, with a link to our site.

Blogs

Blogs are a good way of adding fresh content to your site on a regular basis. You can highlight when news items relate to your products or services – if a well-known celeb is seen using something that you sell, for example, and benefit when people search for the news item or celeb name. You can integrate a blog to your site using something like www.wordpress.org, or have a stand-alone blog. There are benefits to both: a stand-alone blog will provide incoming links to your site, whereas an integrated blog will allow easy updating and addition of new content, both helping your search engine rankings. I do both! I also run the content from my blog onto my Facebook and MySpace pages, and on business networking sites Women's Marketing Forum, Webmums and GiantPotential.

I blog several times a week, depending on other commitments. In an ideal world I'd post at least every day. Sometimes, I note down blog ideas as they come to me through the week then write them up on a Monday. This saves time, and also means that I'm rarely short of ideas. The blog I use allows me to time the posts so they pop up throughout the week. I also add in newsy items and stories as I see them each day. Keep your blog fresh and full of content likely to appeal to your customers and it will get them coming back to read and browse.

Here are some blog providers to get you started:

- www.blogger.com
- www.typepad.com
- www.livejournal.com
- www.blog.co.uk
- www.wordpress.org – download blogging software to enable you to host a blog on your own website – see www.acpr.co.uk/pr-blog for an example
- www.wordpress.com – alternatively have an external blog hosted for you by Wordpress – see www.antoniachitty.wordpress.com

Finally, look at how you tie all your social networking, blogging and other websites together. There are hundreds of tools to allow your new blog posts to appear on your Facebook site and as Tweets, for example. This spreads everything you do to the widest possible audience. Have a look at Friendfeed.com as a good place to start linking up feeds from various sites.

I hope this has given you some ideas to get started. Pick one way to promote your business online each day, and spend a few minutes on it: little and often is the way to get there! Do not be daunted by all the ideas in this chapter – just keep on at it, and tick things off as you do them.

Online Promotion and Attracting Customers: Exercise

Now you have come up with some thoughts on how you plan to set up your website you need to look in more depth at creating content that attracts and retains customers, plus the all important search engine optimisation.

Keywords and phrases

What keywords and phrases are you going to target for your site? Jot down some ideas here. There is more about this in *A Guide to Promoting Your Business*.

Text and formatting
- [ ] Are you using your key phrases within your main website content?
- [ ] Is some text in bold?
- [ ] Are all the links and images on your site descriptive?

Visit Website Grader (http://website.grader.com) and pick out three areas where you could improve your site rating.

1

2

3

Sign up to these sites for more links back to your website
- [ ] You Tube
- [ ] Digg
- [ ] Del.icious
- [ ] Aboutus
- [ ] DMOZ
- [ ] Yahoo
- [ ] Zoominfo
- [ ] GoogleBase
- [ ] GoogleLocal

Set up an Adwords campaign
Draft out your initial ad ideas here. You are limited to three lines, with 25 characters on the top line, 35 on the second and third lines and a URL, You may want to have several attempts and can rotate different versions of an ad. Then, go to https://adwords.google.com to upload your ad.

Here is an example of two of mine:

Maternity Leave Over?	Family Friendly Working
Get a better work life balance	Get a better work life balance
Start your own home business	Learn your rights to flexible work
www.familyfriendlyworking.co.uk	**www.familyfriendlyworking.co.uk**

Sign up for social networking sites:
- ☐ Create a Facebook page
- ☐ Twitter
- ☐ MySpace
- ☐ BTTradeSpace
- ☐ Bebo

Add your own ideas here

Set up a blog

Create a blogging schedule – which days will you set aside for planning your blog each week?

Where can I get news and updates to inspire my blog posts?

Look at setting up searches on GoogleAlert

Polly Gowers founded charity search engine and donation platform, Everyclick. She has some advice about promoting your business online: "Expect that the majority of the users' journeys start at Google and use that knowledge to your advantage. Invest heavily in SEO and make sure that what you publish online and what your customer is looking for is closely aligned and Google will help you do business. With regards to social media, work very hard at turning your customers into your advocates because word of mouth and recommendation is the best advertising there is."

"Over 50% of Everyclick's business comes through referral – that is an exciting place to be. One of the metrics that we measure the success of the business by is how much referral growth increases."

When it comes to site design, Polly says, "If you have the budget always invest in an internal team that can live and breathe the product. If you have to have it built externally, make sure you own all the systems so you don't have any nasty surprises – sometimes you can get caught out."

"Remember to think about the customer journey and less about your company. Too many websites make visitors work too hard, make life simple for them – consider carefully what it is you want them to do and make it easy for them to do it! Once you have built your site review the customer journey endlessly – you can always make it better and improve conversion rates."

Polly Gowers of Everyclick,
www.everyclick.com

We have learnt that search engines are particularly beneficial in that they allow us to target customers very specifically. We have worked extensively to improve our natural rankings ourselves and have learnt how to improve them the hard way, making several time consuming mistakes along the way!

Well, 14 months since the idea to start up as an online nursery furniture and baby bedding retailer was born around the kitchen table, we are trading and sales are increasing as our name gets known. I have become an expert in managing our website and improving its rankings. Editing the website to make it appear in Google and Yahoo naturally, Google Adwords and PR has become our main route to getting customers in. We have tested various forms of advertising along the way. We have learnt that search engines are particularly beneficial in that they allow us to target customers very specifically. By this, I mean that if we sell nursery furniture, we are able to make sure that people searching for nursery furniture can find us. We have worked extensively to improve our natural rankings ourselves and have learnt how to improve them the hard way, making several time consuming mistakes along the way! The good thing is that we now better understand how search engines work and can optimise our website's potential at zero cost. We also use Adwords to enable us to advertise more broadly, although there is certainly some skill involved in choosing the best keywords here. It is easy to select a broad phrase that will most likely have hundreds of clicks, but it will cost a fortune and equate to no sales.

Christianne James, of 4little1s,
www.4little1s.com

Attracting customers online in our experience has been reliant on lots of offline activity such as baby shows, trade shows and exhibitions! We spend a lot of time at shows and events that enable us to show off our range of unique and unusual gifts for newborn babies and mums in person and to explain what they are and how we work. In doing so we talk to thousands of people and each one gets a leaflet and is told how to order online. We give prospective dads and grandparents one of our business cards and tell them to put them in their wallet (most do while with us!) that way we know they will have our details with them when their baby arrives or should they want to tell anyone else about us.

Often, people are very nervous of shopping online especially for a very important event and with an unknown company. Going to events and having eye to eye contact enables them to really get to know who they are dealing with, you are no longer just out there in cyberspace!

Activity like this means that when they see us online, on search engines or through any other promotion that we do, they recognise us... they know us!

Lisa Roberts of BabyBlooms,
www.babyblooms.co.uk

> Often, people are very nervous of shopping online especially for a very important event and with an unknown company. Going to events and having eye to eye contact enables them to really get to know who they are dealing with, you are no longer just out there in cyberspace!

Chapter 8 More Ways to Find Customers

It is what every new business needs to know, isn't it? How do you find customers, and then more customers?

If you have started your business by selling to friends and family, or even if you have lots of virtual mates from a forum busy buying your products, at some point you are going to need to know how to take it to the next level.

Referrals

First, let's start off with the easy stuff. If you have a few customers who like your products and services, get them to start working for you. Offer incentives to recommend your business, such as a discount on their next order. In your newsletter, make sure you include a 'forward to a friend' button. Put flyers in with every order you send out or offer a loyalty card for them to return each time they make a repeat purchase.

Affiliate schemes

An affiliate scheme is simply a way of making this process a little more official. You create a set of links that your affiliates can include in their email signature or on a website. Each time someone clicks and buys through this link, they get a small commission. You can recommend your affiliate programme to customers and they can see a way to earn money. It can work on complementary websites too.

You can find software to create your own affiliate programme or use something like Clickbank to manage it for you. Other affiliate networks include CommissionJunction.com, LinkShare.com, or IncentaClick.com. There are pros and cons to each method. You need more technical knowledge to create your own software, or the help of someone techy, but you will have more control over who signs up. You will need to sort out the legal requirements and membership criteria too. With an affiliate provider like Clickbank you get the benefit of their high search engine ranking when anyone is looking to sign up to affiliate schemes.

Example

I have an affiliate link to AutoresponsePlus – software which can deliver e-courses to your inbox. I have found it easy to use and it gets me good results so I recommend it to clients. Each time someone clicks on www.autoresponseplus.com/link.php?a=antonia which I have in my email signature and my signature on various forums, and goes on to buy the software, I earn a few dollars. The creator of AutoresponsePlus still gets the bulk of the money, plus the benefit of my recommendation. Other businesses use the same idea to sell anything from T-shirts to calendars.

Party plan and direct selling

As well as maximising your affiliate sales, have you thought of taking on people to host parties for you? Setting up this sort of scheme will allow you to extend your reach by taking on self-employed agents who sell your products in return for commission. It allows you to grow your business and reach more customers, and is best suited to businesses selling consumer goods.

To get started with a party plan scheme, you may want to have a trial run with one person, to see how it works. Look at other big direct selling businesses like Avon to see what you can learn. You will need to set up a legal arrangement explaining the agent's responsibilities to you and your responsibilities to them. Think about their starter pack, which will need to include enough samples to entice people to buy. You will need to set a price for this pack that will cover your costs yet make getting started affordable. The pack could also include order forms, catalogues displaying further items and promotional leaflets and flyers to help your agents promote their parties. If you think that door-to-door selling will make up a significant part of the business you will need to have more catalogues and order forms so your agent can leave them with people.

Party plan for your business

Roberta Jerram, founder of online networking forum for women, Giant Potential, has been working in direct sales for almost 20 years and runs a consultancy offering advice to businesses looking to create a party plan scheme. She explains some of the advantages of party plan, *"'Party Plan' is becoming big business with over 9 million people buying at home sales parties each year in the UK. Many large companies over recent years have seen the benefit of utilising direct selling as a way to move their products. They've recognised the potential to reach more customers by recruiting a sales force of independent agents running their own business from home."*

If you're already offering a range of appealing, affordable products in your business then it's probably scalable (ie it could grow beyond being just you). A party plan scheme could be a terrific way to expand a small business and, as a mum yourself, you'll relate to other mums' needs to earn a flexible income and will probably be more in touch with the needs of your customers than the big corporate companies!

- If you love what you do, others will too
- No wages to pay, your sales agents would all be self-employed
- You only pay out commissions based on actual sales results
- You'd gain customers you wouldn't have reached working on your own
- Make a difference: many women out there are looking for flexible earnings
- Keep it simple: most agents want an easy business that fits around their family.

If you think that party plan would fit well with your business, here are Roberta's suggestions for the first steps to take, *"Before recruiting others, be prepared to run some parties yourself first. You will gain first-hand knowledge of your top-selling products and experience the unique dynamics of selling in a group environment. If you've walked the walk it will gain you credibility when it comes to training others. You may prefer to keep things fairly small and local to keep it manageable or decide you want to grow your business into a large household name. Either way, seek out advice from professionals such as consultants, solicitors and accountants who have experience in the direct selling industry, particularly party plan."*

Ten things to think about:

- Commission structure
- Terms & conditions/legal documents
- Starter kit contents
- Operations
- Ordering and admin processes
- Hostess incentives
- Printed literature
- Shipping
- Website
- USP and marketing strategies.

Roberta continues, *"Party plan is all about people, so effective training is crucial. You need to ensure the name of your business is safe in the hands of the people who join you and that they're spreading your message and running their businesses the way you want it to be done. It's usually the people out in the field that can give your business the edge so ensure your agents feel well-supported or they will leave faster than you can recruit them."*

"In addition to organising training and company events, as the business owner it's important you are the one researching the industry, staying ahead of your competitors and refining your unique selling point. Develop your product range to stay on top of your game and, if you've big ambitions to grow a large network of agents across the country, be prepared to invest money in stock, a place to store it and employ 'head office' people to act as your support team. If you don't employ people, the

business will not grow. It won't just sit there either: it will begin to implode under the weight of all that undone work."

"As time goes on, be prepared for your role to evolve into something more managerial in nature. To make it a big success the three golden 'D' rules are, in my opinion:

1 Devote more of your personal time to working on the business rather than in the business.
2 Develop great leadership skills.
3 Delegate."

"As the business owner, set SMART goals, understand your own capabilities, strengths and weaknesses and know what deeply motivates you as a person."

"Whether you want a small or a big business and whether you're more motivated by personal gratification or financial gain, before you launch a party plan scheme, be absolutely certain about what you're taking on and that you understand your profit margins. The financial outlay for this sort of project, even on a small, local scale should not be underestimated. You'll also need to have a lot of time and personal energy at your disposal to do what's required and to deal with the people in your organisation. There will inevitably be more overheads than you can anticipate and if you fail to plan cashflow effectively or don't get good advice, the entire project's failure could potentially take out several other women's incomes as well as your own. Therefore it's important to do the maths first and get some sound advice on the subject. That said, I'm a great advocate of 'nothing ventured, nothing gained' and believe that an entrepreneur with a passion for success is a force to be reckoned with!"

Roberta concludes, "Think about your current product range and if you can tick all of these boxes and want to expand, do consider party plan.

* Are my products affordable to most people?
* Do I have a USP?
* Do I offer goods that aren't easy to find on the high street or in a supermarket?
* Would the items benefit from demonstration in a fun, friendly home environment?

* After purchasing at a party, is a guest likely to want more from the range on another occasion?
* Can I think of incentives to encourage guests to be a hostess of a subsequent party?"

Setting up a party plan scheme

Setting up a scheme like this can be more complex than you think. You need to consider how fast you want to grow and how you will handle the possibility of hundreds of agents all selling your products. Talk to the Direct Selling Association, www.dsa.org.uk, which can offer advice and assistance in creating contracts for your independent, self-employed sales agents. Roberta Jerram offers free consultations to business owners exploring the possibilities of party plan. You can also visit her website, www.robertajerram.co.uk for a newsletter about setting up party plan schemes and a free directory of UK professionals with experience in direct selling. The directory is an up to date list of UK Consultancy companies, Public Liability Insurers and Solicitors who can help draw up your legal documents as well as Business Development Advisors, Trainers, DSA contacts and also an extensive list of recommended reading to save you time and thousands of pounds in costly mistakes.

Getting ready for wholesaling

If you want to expand your business, wholesaling may appeal. You can shift far larger numbers of products if you have a range of outlets selling your product for you. A number of issues need to be sorted out if you want to wholesale.

If you are selling increased volumes, how will you ensure that you can manufacture enough to meet demand? Whether you make a product and are looking for one or two more shops to sell it, or already use a factory and are looking for UK wide distribution, think what would happen if demand doubled. And what if it doubled again? This may seem like your ideal situation, but think of the fall out if you got a fabulous wholesale order but could not supply it, or if the standard of your product fell because you had to create increased volumes.

If you need a manufacturer, talk to your local enterprise agency. Look in local directories or search industrial estates for companies near you.

Remember, the closer the manufacturer, the lower the delivery costs. You may have some success looking online, and this is certainly the way to find out about overseas manufacturers. If you are considering using an overseas manufacturer, remember that you may need to phone them at odd hours or even visit them. Websites such as www.alibaba.com will help you to find companies overseas.

Remember that you may need to improve packaging if your products are being shipped far and wide, and you will need to consider how the products will stand up to the distribution process.

Next, you need to develop a robust pricing structure. You need to take the cost of the manufactured item, and estimate costs for delivery, packaging and promotion. Remember to allocate a proportion of on-costs including your premises, staff and office essentials. Don't forget your own profit! Then, you need to look at how much an item would retail for if you added 30-50% on top of this price that you have come up with. Most retailers want 30-50% profit from an item, although this will vary by sector. Will this bring your item's price in line with other similar products in the market? What would happen if a retailer asked for a large discount – would you still make enough profit?

Once you have researched your production and distribution processes, you need to start looking for buyers. Large businesses will have full-time buyers who look for different products at different times of year. If you have a seasonal product remember that they will be working many months ahead. As one example it may be too late to sell your Christmas products to buyers as early as July!

Create a list of outlets to target and do some detective work to find the name of the buyer. Ask their office when they might consider looking at your sort of products and what information they need. Be prepared to send samples, give presentations and provide details of the promotion you do for your product. Depending how confident you are you may want to target some smaller retailers first and build up. Other business owners decide that this is the time to take on staff with experience of wholesaling and pitching to buyers.

Franchising

Perhaps you have thought of franchising your business. This means setting up a package allowing franchisees to buy into a successful business. They get the right to set up their own version of what you offer: you give them support and systems. Most people looking for a franchise want the benefit of a recognised brand, so you would need to ensure that your business is both known and desirable before embarking on offering franchises. You will also support franchisees with advertising, marketing and PR. You will offer them training and support, and may have in house accounts and business systems that they have to use. Potential franchisees will find your offering more attractive if you can also provide discounts and savings on things such as insurance.

Jane Hopkins of www.mumsclub.co.uk advises, *"A franchise is defined as 'an agreement by which a business or company gives someone the right to market its products in an area; [or]… the area concerned'. The area in which you are given a licence to trade is known as a territory."*

"A territory can be exclusive or non-exclusive and could range from a single postcode to a town, city or even county. Exclusive territories mean no other franchisees are permitted to sell in that area, which can be a key advantage. Franchisors will charge a one-off start up fee, which can range from a small initial investment up to tens of thousands of pounds. Some franchisors will require a percentage of turnover (sales, rather than profits) or may instead charge an annual licence fee. Annual fees may pay towards continual development of the brand, the services and products. The royalty fee is also often used for ongoing training of the franchisees and their staff. There may be other fees associated with a franchise, along with the requirement to purchase equipment and supplies from the franchisor."

More Ways to Find Customers: Exercise

In this section, pick one or two ways to promote your business which look like they will work well for your type of business, explore what is needed to set them up, and test them out.

Create a referral scheme

What incentives could you offer to customers to recommend your business?

How will you promote this to customers?

☐ Newsletter

☐ Flyers

Your ideas:

How much will the incentives cost you? Remember that you need to take this off the profit you make from any recommendations.

Affiliate schemes

Look for software to help you create an affiliate scheme:

• Clickbank

• CommissionJunction.com

• LinkShare.com

• IncentaClick.com

• My own software

How will you promote the scheme and get people to sign up? Remember, you are probably looking for loyal customers who love your products as well as those looking to boost their income.

You may also need to create a contract with your affiliates which they agree to when signing up for the scheme.

TWO MINUTE TIP

Think about whether these are suitable ways to increase your reach, or browse through the resources and downloads at www.prbasics.co.uk to find more ways to reach customers and grow your business.

Party plan and direct selling

Ask your solicitor about legal arrangements for this. Contact the Direct Selling Association for advice.

What will you include in your starter pack?	Total cost of producing the pack:
☐ Samples ☐ Order forms ☐ Catalogues ☐ Promotional leaflets	Price to sellers:

How will you reach potential sellers?

Market your opportunity to happy customers who love your product. You will need to look beyond this group too. Look for websites appealing to part-time workers and mums at home for recruitment such as:

- www.jobs4mothers.com
- www.remoteemployment.com
- www.sliversoftime.com
- www.workingmums.co.uk

- www.mumandworking.co.uk
- www.shiftshack.com
- www.ten2two.org
- www.yummymummyjobs.com

What is your advertising budget to help you promote your opportunity?

Wholesaling First, work out your possible wholesale cost. Do some research to see if this is realistic and will allow both you and your retailers to make a good profit. **Pricing structure** Cost of the manufactured item Costs for delivery Costs for packaging Costs for promotion On-costs including your premises, staff and even office essentials Your profit Total cost to you (A) Possible retail price (B) Possible profit to retailer = B-A Percentage profit (B-A)/B*100	Create a list of outlets to target:

I made the decision not to dropship my Baby Feeding Wheels a while ago, and have stuck to it, despite requests because I just think it won't work for such inexpensive items like mine. What I've done instead is keep the minimum wholesale order amount very low (just £21, ie 12 wheels) so businesses can try the product without a big outlay.

I think if I dropshipped there wouldn't be any incentive for businesses to market or push the wheels, whereas if they are holding some stock there is more incentive to get sales. Plus, online companies who attend fairs and shows can take the wheels with them, which helps get them 'out there'.

As far as wholesale goes, as soon as I had the products, although I was selling them through my own website, I approached some local card and gift shops, and had a really great response, which made me realise that there was potential to sell wholesale. The business is now 95% wholesale sales, I would say, helped by attending trade shows, registering on wholesale supplier websites, sending PRs and receiving mentions in trade magazines, and having trade information including a trade enquiry form on my website.

Elizabeth Geldart of Chiggs
www.chiggs.co.uk

In the early days I did all my sales trips on my moped with all the samples of our range of bags, purses and the 'trolley-dolly' in my rucksack. The sight of me in a luminous yellow coat and helmet was enough to scare some lovely stores in to buying our products. Liberty of London was my first stockist followed shortly by Heals, Harrods, Selfridges, Fortnum and Mason. You have to pick the shops which can take the price you will have to charge and suit your image. You don't want to be in Superdrug if you sell Prada face cream. I know the market has changed hugely but it is still important when establishing yourself.

I had to persevere to get meetings with buyers. My advice is to ring and ring and ring. Make sure you send photos and estimate price points so that when you ring they have something to look at. I don't believe email is enough any more either. I started before email existed en masse so I had to send things to the buyers by post. It is more expensive but a random email will just be deleted or ignored. Make sure you find out when buyers for certain stores will be looking for new products as they all differ. Think about seasons and what you are selling and when it will arrive, make sure you can deliver when they want it too.

My final tip is to say remember it is a slow process. Try and keep a record of all the good stuff – a press book, prizes and things. Then when there are down days, bad payments, problems to overcome these will remind you how far you have come. Set goals for 2-3 years, a year and then right down to tomorrow… and write them down. And finally ALWAYS ask – ask for help and ask for feedback.

Zoe Phayre-Mudge, of ZPM,
www.zpm.com

I put lots of thought into the background information and developed an e-course and telephone training for everyone who signs up. The initial materials for the agents have cost me around £1000. I decided to offer very high commissions as I wanted to give sellers a proper reward.

I spent a long time planning and researching my affiliate scheme for Arabella Miller, my organic baby clothing store. I looked at what other people had done and saw other people were using them, but I wasn't sure how it all worked. I checked out different schemes and joined affiliate.org. It was not easy to get the software working with my shopping cart. I found it incredibly fiddly. The script generated a unique code which would be remembered for something like three months so the original referrer would get around 8% of sales for that period. It now seems really easy, but it took a lot of testing to get it to run properly. In hindsight, I would have set up a scheme that is also accepted by sites such as Quidco.

I also use party plan to promote Arabella Miller. It all happened because a customer who had been with me from the beginning said that she sold my T-shirts to a friend and also wanted to run stalls selling them. I checked out other party plan schemes and got information from the people who were running them. I researched terms and conditions for the plan. I got them checked by BusinessLink. I put lots of thought into the background information and developed an e-course and telephone training for everyone who signs up. The initial materials for the agents have cost me around £1000. I decided to offer very high commissions as I wanted to give sellers a proper reward. It works out at 50%: 40% up front and a 10% bonus.

There are three kits on offer: babies, children or both. I have aimed to make the kits affordable, but not cheap. I need to ensure that people work to earn their initial investment back. There is no choice of sample sizes to deter people from buying just for their own kids. I plan in communication to motivate the agents: they get blog updates and stock updates. I have promoted the opportunity through press releases and in places where mums would go – I've spent around £500 advertising on Mumsnet, Netmums and Mum and Working. I check with Google Analytics to see if the right people are coming through.

In the first few months of the scheme I attracted around 10 agents. I know that, because of the nature of the people who this will appeal to, there will be those who stop: one of my keenest agents has just had a baby. For me, it is another sales channel, but not one I rely on for regular sales at the moment.

Alison Rothwell of Arabella Miller,
www.arabellamiller.com

Chapter 9 Looking After Your Life

When you start your own business, you will find you are pouring all your spare time, energy and resources into your fledgling enterprise. After a while, though, you may realise that your business has taken over from the time you used to spend relaxing or with your partner.

Putting everything into the business can be done for a while: it can even be necessary to create a successful start up. But, without looking after yourself and taking care of your relationships you will soon run out of steam and start resenting the business. This part of *The Mumpreneur Guide's Start Your Own Business* book will help you work out all the different factors you need to juggle to keep home and work running smoothly.

Dealing with childcare

The most important thing for many mumpreneurs is to get the childcare right. Look at your plans for your business, and think about when you are going to fit the work in. Many mums start their business when they have a baby. Initially, if the baby sleeps a lot you may find you can fit in quite a lot during the day. However, over the months as naps become fewer, you will find yourself working into the evenings and over the weekends to keep up. Few people can run a successful business relying on working in the evening or weekend alone in the long term, although you may start out this way. And when you are looking after a small baby and getting disturbed nights you need some down time. If not, you can end up feeling extremely tired and run down as you are using all your spare time and relaxation time to work, as well as looking after the baby all day.

However, even though babies nap less as they grow, they also start to become more interested in playing alongside others. Talk to other mums as now may be the time to start doing a 'baby swap'. You could take her baby and yours to the park one morning, and she could have your child round to play another day. Mums are always in a need of a little time to themselves, so this idea will also appeal to mums who don't have a growing business to develop.

Do you have friends or family who could take your child out for an hour or two? If grandparents are local they may be happy to set up a regular afternoon to take care of your child or you may be able to persuade dad that you would like part of the weekend as work time.

Once your child reaches two or three, you will find plenty of playgroups that they can attend. It may seem a wrench to leave them for a couple of hours, but it will help them socialise and you will be amazed how much you can get done. You could also look into paid childcare. A childminder or nursery can prove invaluable if you want to take a more formal approach to work.

Schooltime

Mums with school age children will have an easier job to fit work in as they have from nine in the morning until pick up at three. However you need to remember that, unless you have an exceptionally supportive partner, everyone will still assume that you are doing all the shopping, washing and cleaning. If you have been a stay at home mum for some years, friends will think you are available for coffee whenever they want to drop in. Try to make sure everyone is clear that you are starting a business. It may seem slightly artificial but setting your 'working hours' can help you know when to start work and when to stop. If you find it hard to make the transition from working on your business to listening to the kids' concerns at the end of the day, make a point of stopping work at 2.30, and spend half an hour winding down, doing a few chores or having a cup of tea.

Another thing to note about working for yourself is that it is likely that you will still be the one who is called upon if a child is sick. Work out contingency plans for unexpected days when your child cannot go to nursery or school. Do you have a friend or family member who could cover certain days? How flexible is your partner's job? Or do you need to sign up to a website like www.emergencychildcare.co.uk which offers nannies at short notice.

You may even want to set a morning or day each week as your 'home day'. I currently work Monday, Wednesday and Friday. On other days, I take my sons to Tumbletots and Friday we stay at home, visit friends or go to the library. That way I don't feel like I'm missing out on being a stay at home mum too: if I wanted to work every day of the week nine until five I could have stayed in employment.

Partners

As you go into business, it will really help if you keep your partner on board and enthusiastic. He, or she, may not realise quite what you are planning, and become resentful and unsupportive if they suddenly find that you spend every evening tucked away in the workshop or office. You may well need their support at busy times, if only to help packing or look after the kids while you do an emergency post office run.

Make time to listen when your partner talks about their work, and tell them about the progress you are making with the business. Alongside this, make time to do the things you both enjoy. You could use the proceeds from your first income to go out for a meal together, for example, so your partner can see the positive things that come from the business.

Other help with the business

Many mums find that their businesses grow to the stage where they need a little help. Taking on a member of staff can seem impossible, especially if you are at the stage where you are investing heavily in the business and taking little pay yourself. There are ways round this, though. If you need help with basic tasks like packing or taking parcels to the post office you may be able to take on a casual worker. This could be a local teen or a mum from school: someone who wants a few hours of occasional work. If you are

running your business from home you may feel weird about having someone working in your house, but it is a good way to free you up for other jobs. Write down a list of the tasks you want the person to do. Check out the Inland Revenue website for guidelines on employing casual or self-employed workers.

Another way to make your business work more efficiently may be to contract out part of the work to a freelancer. This is when it makes sense to look at your weak points. If you struggle with the web, you could find someone to help maintain and run your website. If figures are not your forte, simply put all your sales, bills and receipts into an envelope each week and get a bookkeeper to tally up the totals. You could also employ a virtual assistant, someone to do your PR, write copy and design your promotional literature: just think about what would be most useful to you.

'Me time'

So, you've got the business started, you have arranged to work when the children are occupied, your partner is on board and supportive, but you still feel drained. Many mums spend so much time caring for everyone else that they leave little time to look after themselves. Any spare moments tend to be taken up by the business.

So, how do you create a little 'me time' as part of your busy routine? Firstly, set some time aside. I mentioned earlier about deciding on your working hours, and you probably have fixed times to collect the children, give them tea and put them to bed. Well, somewhere in there, set aside a couple of hours for yourself. Could you pop into the swimming pool after the school drop-off once a week? Or finish an hour early and go and meet a friend for a coffee and a gossip every Friday. Perhaps you might like to join a book group, take part in your local NCT or make regular time for a massage. If it is hard to get out in the evenings, make one night a week your 'pamper night' where you have a long luxurious bath and paint your toenails. Whatever way you relax, make time to do it. You and your family will benefit.

Looking After Your Life: Exercise

What are the important things in your life?

The exercise for this Chapter is relatively simple, and is all about working out your life priorities – ie what is important to you. Go back and look at why you wanted to run your own business in the first place. Was it to do with control over your time – getting enough time for the family and working when it fitted in well with family routines? Write down a few of your key aims:

Now think about some of the elements of your life that you would like to get into balance. I have made some suggestions and write in your own ideas.

Health	Money	Your own suggestions
Time with the kids	Relationship	
Finances	Friends	
Time to yourself	Exercise	
Spirituality	Creativity	

Pick your eight priorities, and give each a score out of 10 for how content you are at the moment, with 0 meaning very unhappy, and 10 meaning totally content. Plot these out on the circle below to get a picture of areas to prioritise in order to get your life in balance.

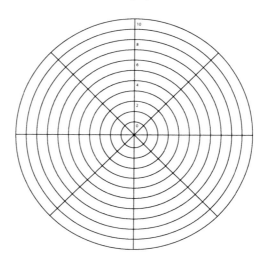

Now pick one or maybe two areas to work on. Write down a goal, not something vague like 'set aside more time for me', but instead something specific such as 'spend every Friday lunchtime having lunch with a friend'. Make your goals achievable and realistic. We might all like monthly spa breaks but that is one goal I'm certainly unlikely to achieve.

My goals:

Then, you may want to look at the steps you need to take to achieve that goal. Work out barriers that are stopping you too. You may think, "I can't meet people for lunch as my toddler always plays up". Work out ways to overcome the barriers – could you do a playdate swap to create the time for a nice adult lunch, or would you prefer to find a venue with a play area if your friend also has a pre-schooler? You may also want to put in positive steps, such as 'block out space every Friday in my diary' and 'ring friends to arrange lunch at the start of every month'.

My barriers:

Steps I can take to overcome these barriers. If you find it difficult to work this out, think what advice you might give to a friend in the same situation. Could this apply to you?

Positive steps I need to take to achieve my personal goals:

You may want to come back and do this for another part of your life in a few months' time. If your goal is relatively manageable you may decide to work on two areas at once.

My goal:

My barriers:

Steps I can take to overcome them:

Positive steps I need to take to achieve my personal goals:

I am currently trying to raise two small girls and run a new business! My goodness me, I never understood the idea of 'having it all – wanting it all' before now but I have such admiration for those women who really strive to give everything in their lives 100%. I will be the first to admit that I am not really at that point yet but I am learning – and fast!

There are a few practical things that I have put into place so that the time I do have at home is not filled up with household tasks – I am now a convert to online shopping – everything is bought online! I make lists all the time, one for work issues and one for home life. I stock up on birthday presents and birthday cards and try to fill up the freezer with as many 'ready to go' meals as I can (I have been caught out and have had to stop for a couple of happy meals on some occasions though – I admit it!).

I use my family and friends as much as I can both with juggling the children and with work issues if they are able to help and then I try to repay the favour – everyone I know at the moment is crazily busy so having a network around you makes sense.

The most difficult part is turning off the Blackberry when I am 'off duty', there doesn't seem to be such a thing as a day off when you have your own business. I find myself sneakily checking my emails when I am supposed to be watching High School Musical or making rice krispie cakes!

I have become more strict with myself now and although it is difficult, I try to draw the line between home time and work time.

I also believe in spending some time away from the office – particularly when it is in your own home. I actually schedule in time to go to the gym and book hair appointments way in advance so that six months do not go past and then I suddenly realise that my hair resembles that of a scare-crow! The key, however boring it may sound, is to be super-organised.

I am passionate about my new business – so many of our clients are busy working mums which is exactly why I know what they are looking for when they come to one of our boot camps. Sometimes you need someone else to do the thinking for you so that you can just ...be!

I also love being a mum to Maisie and Lola and I don't want to compromise their childhood and miss out on all the wonderful things they are learning and doing. It is a juggling act and sometimes I drop the balls!

Sam Watts of Ultimate Boot Camp,
www.ultimatebootcamp.co.uk

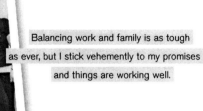

> Balancing work and family is as tough as ever, but I stick vehemently to my promises and things are working well.

In 2003 my sister, Anna, moved from Harpenden to Amsterdam and joined 'The Little Gym Amsterdam' with her son Tom (then two). I visited fairly often and was welcome to join in Tom's 'Boefjes (Super-Beasts) class'. It was a parent/child class as the boys were under three and I remember being wow-ed by the welcome from the team, the clean colourful environment and the fun class in which I was encouraged to actively participate with my son Sam.

I remember thinking 'if only there was a 'The Little Gym' in Harpenden or St Albans'... little did I know that five years later there would be... and I would be the franchise owner!

My background is in accountancy, I worked for over 13 years for Ernst & Young, first in London and then Luton. I really enjoyed it and appreciated the flexibility they gave me during the early years with my boys, Sam and George. However, NCT classes introduced me to Harpenden locals and I felt a growing desire to be part of my community and not just a commuter.

Eventually I gathered the courage to resign and start my new journey. On day one I wrote the following promises on a poster in my makeshift office, and these have guided me ever since:

· I will make time every day to stop, think and plan
· Sam and George will get Mummy work and play time every day
· I will continue to support Ed in his work and "Ed time"
· I will go to the gym twice a week
· I will make a difference to children and parents in the community
· I will use my network and give back to my network

Balancing work and family is as tough as ever, but I stick vehemently to my promises and things are working well.

Lindsey Venner of The Little Gym Harpenden,
www.thelittlegym.co.uk

The struggle between running a family and a business is very, very hard – physically and mentally. My husband, although supportive of our project still expected a tidy home, childcare organised and a full fridge. Sadly our marriage is now over and although I would not want my business which sells fun, reusable stickers for kids' rooms, FunToSee, to be totally at blame for this, it has certainly played a significant part. Now, a single mum, I have my own small home and I have even more drive to succeed as I have to support myself and my boys. Being a working mum means life is extremely hectic and 'my time' is rare, as any working mum knows… keeping in touch with friends, going to the gym, trying to look after my sick father, the list goes on. Until recently we were not paying ourselves a salary so even when I did have time, funds were short to do much. That is fortunately slowly changing as we now draw a salary.

My children have only ever known their mother as a working mum. From one month Johnnie would come to meetings with me in his little rocking chair, or I would be rocking his chair with one foot whilst getting an artwork job done. They are both now at school, but I find the hardest times are the school holidays. I need to work but I also want to make their holidays fun and memorable. If I take time off to be with them I feel guilty that my colleague Rachel is working, or if I am working I feel guilty that I am not with them. They won't want to play with me forever and I really want to make the most of those moments now.

I share childcare with the boys' father – I have them four days a week and he has them for three. We both have to travel with work sometimes so are both flexible. This arrangement means that I can be a dedicated mum four days a week and then have three days a week to be at work early, if required, plan meetings without the worry of them running over and being late to collect from school, and have time to catch up with friends.

Louise Dutton, Founder of FunToSee,
www.FunToSee.com

My children have only ever known their mother as a working mum. From one month Johnnie would come to meetings with me in his little rocking chair, or I would be rocking his chair with one foot whilst getting an artwork job done. They are both now at school, but I find the hardest times are the school holidays. I need to work but I also want to make their holidays fun and memorable.

My husband's job requires that we move about every three years, and we can get assigned just about anywhere. He has about nine years left before we can retire from this position, which means another three or four moves minimum. I started my own online retail business selling practical and stylish baby products for mums and dads because it is portable. Once we leave the UK, I will turn our inventory over to a fufillment company, and keep the business going wherever we move next. The advantage of moving so much is the ability to see what is selling well in one market and take it to the next. The disadvantage is that sometimes it is hard to really plan long range when we don't know where we are moving next.

As far as work life balance goes with the children, I will be the first to admit that I don't always get it right. I think the biggest part of getting balance is to know when to ask for help. Recently, I went through a miscarriage that pretty much knocked me off of my feet. Without family around, it was important to have a support network of friends that I could ask for help with kids, meals, etc. The same friends have also helped at stressful points in the business.

I also have found that I need help with the cleaning. I know not everyone can afford it, but I have housekeepers come in. I scrimp everywhere else in our budget for them to come, but it is worth it. Their cleaning allows me to have more time with family and with the business.

Elisabeth Webber of Baby Soleil,
www.baby-soleil.com

As far as work life balance goes with the children, I will be the first to admit that I don't always get it right. I think the biggest part of getting balance is to know when to ask for help

> The key to family survival is to make 'you time' as valued as possible, half an hour of 'quality time' is as valued as a whole day of 'just being there'.

There is enough work at work to occupy all the waking hours; there is enough going on at home to occupy all the waking hours. So how can you get a quart into a pint pot? The key to business survival is to keep your costs as low as possible. The key to family survival is to make 'you time' as valued as possible, half an hour of 'quality time' is as valued as a whole day of 'just being there'.

It's easy enough to let work take over your life in a normal climate, but when a recession hits and you are literally fighting for survival, it not only affects your time but your attitude to your whole life. Prioritising is not easy, but letting things that can wait, wait, will allow you time to play a game or just have a reassuring chat with your children.

When you are at work it is strangers that are demanding your time. When you are at home it's your loved ones who are asking to share your time. 'Me time' has to be slotted in between the working hours but can involve family life and it is important to take your mind to a happy place.

'Me time' is a state of mind and can be reached with the simplest of actions, watching a favourite tv programme in bed before going to sleep or simply reading a book can all aid this process. You must always be realistic with your time and don't let yourself be bullied by others into stealing family time for work too often.

It is said that the only things in life that are certain are death and taxes, well one is inevitable, and the other, well that is dictated by people no better than ourselves so make your own life work for you and your family.

Nicola Ena-Smith of Organ-nics,
www.organ-nics.com

You may have plans for a small manageable business that you can fit into your spare time. However, lots of mumpreneurs want to make it big with their business.

In this chapter of *The Mumpreneur Guide's Start Your Own Business* book you can find some pointers on how to take your business to the next level and hear from women who have made it big.

Trademarks, registered designs, copyright and patents

If you are going to develop a business of any size you need to be sure that you are building on firm foundations. It is soul-destroying to find that someone else is using a similar branding or producing a product with an identical design, and there are things you can do to protect yourself.

Starting with copyright, this covers information you have written for your website or promotional materials. You automatically have copyright on anything that you write. Keep copies of drafts and notes to show that you are the originator of the material. If you find someone has pinched your written material, you need to write pointing out that it is copyright and they cannot use it without permission. Depending on the situation you may be happy for them to use the text with a credit and link back to your website, for example, or you may want them to remove it altogether. If they do not follow your wishes after a written request, you may want to get advice from your local business adviser, the Federation of Small Businesses or a solicitor.

If you have designed something, you have 12 months from making the product public to register the design with the UK Intellectual Property Office. Look through catalogues, search on the internet, and check existing registered designs to make sure your design is new and unique. You then need to fill in forms from the UKIPO website (www.ipo.gov.uk) to register. It costs around £60 and will protect your design for up to 25 years, renewable every five years.

A patent protects the technical and functional aspects of products and processes. You can apply for a patent if your product is new and inventive. Carry out market research to ensure your invention is commercially viable before investing your time and money, but make sure you get people to sign a confidentiality agreement before you ask for their opinion. Look for other similar ideas through the free online search of registered patents at http://gb.espacenet.com before you apply. The process can take a number of years and involves various payments of between £30 and £100 at the different stages. Prepare a description of your product, drawings, claims for what it does, and a technical summary before you fill in the initial application forms on the UKIPO site. You may then be asked to improve the product information and send in prototypes.

You can trademark the logo, words or images which make your products and services different to those of another company. Make sure your proposed trademark is clearly different to other businesses in similar sectors. Registration costs £200 for one class of goods or services, plus £50 for each further sector.

For more excellent advice about protecting your business ideas, check out *The Bright Idea Handbook* by Michael Gardner (Which? Essential Guides).

Financing your business expansion

So, registering to protect your business can incur costs, even before you start to look at manufacturing, sales costs and promotion. However, there are a number of ways to find finance to grow your business.

Start by talking to your local enterprise agency. There may be grants available in your area. Then, it's off to the bank. If you have a business account and a good relationship with your bank manager you may want to start there: they will ask for a business plan and financial projections. You may find it easier to get a personal loan, but this leaves you personally responsible for the debt. Be cautious if a friend or family member offers to help finance your business as they may also want a say in your business plans.

For those who have registered their business as a company there are more options, and the business is liable for the debt if you struggle with repayments. You can still approach a bank with your business plan. Think about the funds you can invest, and bring along any contracts you have to supply goods or services, to demonstrate where the money will be coming from to repay the loan. If you get a loan you may need to update the bank on a regular basis about your progress.

There are also professional investors called angels. They make a living from investing in a number of businesses and will be very clear about what makes it likely that your business will succeed. You will probably need to give them a part of your business, known as shares or equity, in return for their money. They are likely to have helpful suggestions to improve the way the company works and the profit it makes: as an active investor you will need to heed what they say.

An alternative for those looking for a large amount of money is to approach a venture capitalist. A further type of professional investor, venture capitalists invest hundreds of thousands of pounds in return for a share in the company. You will also have performance targets to meet in this sort of situation.

One final comment from Polly Gowers of www.everyclick.com puts finance in context, *"If you are raising capital always raise twice as much as you think and expect it to take five times as long. It is an extremely time consuming part of the business. What's more, fundraising is so time consuming that it's easy to think once you have raised the money that you are there. Actually that is just the beginning of the journey.'*

Outsourcing

Once you have the finance in place, you can increase your output if you offer a product. You may be making your product yourself: but if you want to make it big you need to think about how you will outsource manufacture. Similarly, if you offer a service, you need to think about how you can increase your capacity to take on more work.

Starting with products, you may have something that can be made by outworkers. There are plenty of people who would like to make items for you on a freelance basis in their own homes. You may need certain skills or require them to make test items. You do not have to contract to supply any particular amount of work, but you will need to set up a system to count the work they do and pay accordingly. Be clear from the outset about the standards the outworkers must achieve.

For a service provider, the equivalent to an outworker could be taking on a freelancer. In the previous part of the book, I mentioned identifying areas where you are weakest and taking on additional virtual assistant (VA) or PR support, for example. You may now want to take on someone to back up your own skills. At times I use PR freelancers in my PR business, ACPR (www.acpr.co.uk) so I can keep up commitments to clients. I usually get someone whose work I know already, or ask them to do a few sessions in my home where I can supervise their work before letting them work more independently in their own home. If you have premises you may want to get a freelancer into your office. If you are using someone on a frequent and regular basis check with the Inland Revenue when a freelancer actually becomes an employee.

Back to products. You may decide that you want to think bigger than outworkers, or prefer to put all your manufacturing in one place. Finding a reliable factory can take considerable research and time. Ask your local enterprise agency for referrals to local manufacturing companies. Check out options for overseas manufacture, which may seem cheaper initially but can come with additional import costs and taxes.

Sales and wholesaling

Alongside setting up plans for increasing the number of products you can provide or the services you can offer, you need to consider how you are going to increase your sales. In previous parts of this book we have looked at ways to promote your business, wholesaling, party plan and franchises. You could also now consider taking on distributors in different countries or licensing your designs for others to make and sell.

Selling up

So, you've put all your effort into growing your business, but the time has come to move on. When you are running a business to fit in with the family, there may come a time when it no longer fits. Many mumpreneurs find that after time a business no longer suits their needs and they look to sell. You may have a great business, but be stuck when it comes to the time that you need to move on.

This can be made much easier if you have put plans in place to sell your business many years before you do so. The way in which you plan this will affect how much you get for the business and how easy it is to sell. If you have invested time and money in growing a business and want to sell up and get something back, here are a few tips and resources:

1   Register as a company. This makes it much easier to sell a business.
2   Maintain good accounts. As a company you have a duty to provide annual accounts. These would be looked at by any potential buyer so that they can assess the value of the company.
3   Remember that good records count. Have your customer databases up to date to prove their value.
4   Get good staff and systems. If the business relies on you entirely, and everything about it is in your head, it will be hard for anyone to take it over.
5   Show that your profits have increased each year, and offer well maintained assets.
6   Take time to find a buyer. If you need to sell in a rush you won't get the best price.

7   Talk to an agent. Even if you think your business is small, it is worth talking to a professional. They can value your business or promote it for sale for you.
8   List your business on the right websites. Potential buyers will be looking on sites like Businesses for Sale.com so find as many sites as you can to list it. You may want to set up a special, anonymous, email address for initial enquiries.
9   Tell everyone about the fact that you are selling up. Word of mouth can be the best way to find a buyer. I'm happy to advertise WAHM businesses for sale in my newsletter and blog: just send me a short para about the business (antonia@acpr.co.uk).
10 Read more at Business Link (www.businesslink.gov.uk). It is a great site to start with, whatever your business issue, and tells you what you need to do to get ready to sell your business.

This section can only give you a few ideas on growing your business: make the most of advice from other women in business who have been there already by visiting some of the online forums I recommended in Chapter One of the book.

I hope your business plans have come on considerably since you started this book. I'd love to hear how things are going. I'm always looking for new businesses to write about so get in touch with me, antonia@acpr.co.uk.

Bigger Business – Taking it to the Next Level: Exercise

There isn't a big exercise for this section, just a question I want you to ask yourself. How far do you want to grow your business? Take some time over the next few days to think this one through for yourself. Note down your thoughts and dreams here. If you decide to turn your dream into a concrete plan to expand your business, make sure you return here every once in a while to make sure your plans are on track.

My dream for my business:

Making your small business into a big one will require commitment and sacrifice. If it is what you want, go for it! Get good advisers on board and aim for your dream.

Gillian founded web design business www.web-feet.co.uk in July 1999 and since then has created over a thousand websites for all types of companies from start-ups to household names. Web-Feet was started at home at a time when Gillian had an eight month old baby, a chronically sick two and a half year old and a 16 year old teenager. Looking back she says, "I don't know how I coped. The first two years were the hardest, trying to establish the business, get orders in and juggle the demands of three children and running a home."

Gillian has always been good at sales, but shied away from cold calling particularly by phone. After missing the Yellow Pages deadline the phone wasn't ringing off the hook and she realised if she didn't conquer her fear she wouldn't have a business. She says, "I quickly mastered telemarketing and the foundations of a good business was born."

After only a year Gillian was looking for premises locally as she already had five staff, and had outgrown the spare bedroom at home. She says, "It was daunting as I now had to sell a certain amount each month to pay rent, rates, etc as well as the salaries." Web-Feet has grown steadily year on year but always at a manageable rate. Four years ago Gillian's husband Stewart was able to give up his high paid corporate job and join the company. This has helped tremendously with taxi-ing the children around. Gillian says, "I know that there is someone with the same ideals as me in the office whilst I am out selling."

Gillian has just introduced a new division of Web-Feet called www.webdesignhampshire.co.uk which gives clients templated designed sites to match most companies' colour schemes and includes hosting, and search engine submissions. She says, "We realised that not all businesses could afford our custom designs so we have created this new service. It has allowed us to go on expanding the business and reach a new group of clients."

Gillian Liesnham of Web-Feet,
www.web-feet.co.uk

In 'The Seven Habits of Highly Effective People' Stephen Covey's second habit is – "Begin with the end in mind" – this is always the advice I give to people when starting up a business. Having a clear and considered, well-thought through vision is vital for success. If you know what you are planning to achieve, then you are less likely to make mistakes and stumble through your journey. I was very clear on what I wanted to achieve with Diva Cosmetics – I knew that I needed to deliver the very best experience for my customers and I knew that I wanted Diva to be recognised as being a leading supplier of in-house colour cosmetics. I didn't realise in those early days exactly what that would entail and this developed as the business grew – but I did understand my passion, my desires and my aims.

I think that passion is one of the most crucial and fundamental states for anyone wishing to work for themselves – regardless of how large or how small the business is going to be. Passion is the differentiation between success and mediocrity. When you work for yourself, you need to be passionate in what you are doing, passionate in why you are doing it, have a passion to want to continually learn and develop and it goes without saying that you also need to have a passion for business, for making money and for providing the best service and experience you possibly can for your customers and your staff.

The other area which I attribute to my success is 'attention to detail'… It was only by constantly reviewing my business and realising and understanding the dependency we had on one particular customer that I was motivated to seek out new customers and embark on a marketing strategy in order to gain at least two new clients. This attention to detail and understanding of my business took me one step closer to achieving my vision of being a leading supplier of in-house cosmetics.

My advice to anyone who aspires to run a national or international business rather than just work from home is to become an expert in your chosen field – be clear on your customers, be clear on the areas which give you stand-out versus the competition, be clear on your pricing and remain focussed (even when the going gets tough). Confidence is key to success – and by knowing and understanding your market – there is absolutely no reason why you cannot make the leap into a national business. Every business started somewhere!

Finally, I didn't start my business with an exit strategy in mind – however when I realised that it was something I wanted to do – I planned it! I made sure that I was no longer the only face of the company (which you strive to do in the early days), I invested in training to ensure that the Diva staff were empowered to work on their own and make their own decisions (in start-ups, so often, the owner/manager makes all decisions – sometimes because s/he wants to – and sometimes because the staff find it easier!) and I discovered that by setting up my company correctly in the first place, I was able to sail through Due Diligence without any major scares. I always advise companies to set themselves up correctly first time around – seek advice from a good solicitor and a good accountant, ensure that HR policies are in place with contracts of employment and of course don't try and cheat any system – it is a false economy. Diva was set up correctly – and when I did sell Diva – I used the same accountant and solicitor – who had been with me throughout the journey – I truly believe that you build your business by building relationships.

Emma Wimhurst of EMpwr,
www.EMpwr.co.uk

When I launched JoJo Maman Bébé in 1993 I had an idea to grow the brand to become a key player in the market. Sixteen years ago there was no internet, but mail order offered the perfect opportunity to scale the business in line with consumer demand. Businesses today have a huge advantage since the costs of implementing a website are nothing compared to producing, printing and mailing a catalogue. However at the time, I felt that mail order gave me the opportunity to reach the niche mother and baby market across the country rather than be confined to the geographical location of one store.

We grew year on year by mail order until about four years ago when we decided that it was time to invest in bricks and mortar. By then there was an abundance of competition by mail order and web and the market was becoming crowded. A newly pregnant woman might get confused online as to which companies are fly by night and which are well established with a good reputation.

It was important for us to permit our customers to feel and touch the clothes and products; hence our high street presence was launched. Our first stores opened in London. In the first year we took our time assessing each location. Not all new locations were a success and we did have to close some of the early stores due to our rents being too high for the potential sales. Retail is not easy, especially with a costly hand built shop fit, plus fit out costs, stock holding and staffing.

Opening stores is extremely costly and obviously in the current economic climate funding is hard to secure. However, we are determined to remain an independent company for as long as possible. Our company ethos is to put a great deal of time and effort into our staff, our customer service and our company charity. These values are expensive and obviously cut into our profit margins. We are determined to pursue our goals to grow the company without diluting our brand ethos, which means we will almost certainly continue to expand organically.

In order to offer an all round service, opening our stores was an important move and one which we have never regretted. We hope to open many more stores across the country and internationally over the next few years.

Laura Tenison of JoJo Maman Bebe,
www.jojomamanbebe.co.uk

Our first stores opened in London. In the first year we took our time assessing each location. Not all new locations were a success and we did have to close some of the early stores due to our rents being too high for the potential sales. Retail is not easy, especially with a costly hand built shop fit, plus fit out costs, stock holding and staffing.

Frugi has grown, from a spare room to a team of 12 based on a lovely organic farm in Cornwall. We really hit the market at the right time with our organic, ethical clothing, and we do have big plans for Frugi in the future.

Frugi is an organic and fair trade online clothing company for children and mums. It began as Cut4Cloth five years ago after I discovered there was a gap in the market for baby clothes tailored to fit over bulkier cloth nappies. We gave ourselves 12 months to see what happened, both giving up our jobs, re-mortgaging the house and putting absolutely everything on the line. We knew that if it was going to give us a proper alternative to our existing salaries, we would have to do things bigger than we actually were – using professional photographers for catalogues for instance. All along we always made a huge effort not to look like the back bedroom business we were – to be taken seriously and to be able to grow quick enough to survive – as we had no other income in the meantime! The internet helped us to source suppliers, market our brand and retail to customers.

Our initial baby collection, from 0-2 years, proved incredibly popular. We knew, during the first couple of years that we could grow to offer older age ranges as customers loved our high quality soft cotton and long lasting clothes. Frugi is now available from newborn to 6 years, and we now have a range of Frugi Mother breastfeeding clothing as well. Our popular designs come from a mum's point of view with a strong focus on great attention to detail - comfy jersey lined waistbands, versatile reversible tops and roll up bottoms, with fresh colourful designs - a real celebration of childhood.

Frugi has grown, from a spare room to a team of 12 based on a lovely organic farm in Cornwall. We really hit the market at the right time with our organic, ethical clothing, and we do have big plans for Frugi in the future. My top tips for mumpreneurs aspiring to grow their business:

- Ensure you have access to good business advice. Business Link and other bodies can be a good source of information and professional contacts
- Plan carefully – in financial terms, product ranges, growth/targets etc
- Organise your time – with increased staff you may have to spend more time actually managing the developing roles
- Keep in touch with all aspects of your growing company - customers, staff, manufacturers and competition
- Sustain your energy and enthusiasm – remember working for yourself can be more demanding but ultimately much more rewarding.

Lucy Jewson of Frugi,
www.welovefrugi.com

We always had international expansion in our business plan for Cuddledry, our baby bathtime products company, but it became clear the moment we launched that it was something that was going to happen fast. We had a huge amount to learn and frankly even the language and abbreviations used in international trade were gobbledeegook to us at that stage.

At Cuddledry we have always made sure we listen, listen, listen – particularly to people at trade shows, who are experienced in our sector and the ways of business within it – and we really applied this to overseas growth. We even travelled to the Netherlands in the very early days of our business and learned a huge amount from someone who wanted to distribute our products over there from the word go. We quickly realised how much information we needed to get together to market our apron towels and our brand effectively overseas, and so we contacted some 'old hands' within the nursery trade and simply asked for their guidance. This helped us prepare what we needed and know what to expect.

One of the tips we were given was becoming part of the Government's 'Passport to Export' scheme, through which we found we could secure grants, and even more importantly, excellent training and consultancy to equip us with the skills and information we needed. We were accepted onto this UKTi scheme in September 2007 and immediately attended our first international trade show. Our consultant wisely advised us not to get overexcited and jump at offers, but to take a measured approach and interview everyone interested in taking our products to their nation or territory. This we did, and on our return to the UK we sat and scored each impartially – taking the emotion out of the decision about who to work with, so we really knew the people we had met had the assets Cuddledry needed.

We attended courses on agents and distributors, and we also undertook a full review of our international communications strategy – even down to looking into the historical influences on trade in each nation we deal with. We have remained on the Passport scheme until very recently, with constant advice and support which has been amazing. We have just 'graduated' on to the new G3 government scheme, which is all about supporting successful businesses as they expand overseas. There is support offered for visits to potential new markets, guidance available at the end of an email or phone, and a host of other benefits. The support of these schemes has given us the confidence to say no quite frequently, thus protecting the integrity of the Cuddledry brand as it expands throughout the world. We currently trade in 30 countries and this extends constantly. We find it hard to believe – that our front room invention is now a global brand and selling worldwide, but it really is, and forms over 25% of our business now.

Helen Wooldridge of Cuddledry,
www.cuddledry.com

What Next?

Thanks for sticking with this book right to the end. I hope that it has given you some useful ideas for your own business. This section of the book is about what to do next.

Take a little time to go back over the sections of the book. Is there one part where you feel like you really haven't got to grips with the subject? Now is the time to remind yourself that you don't have to be expert at everything, and get some help. Talk to your local business adviser if you need help with your business plan.

Start looking for a bookkeeper, PA or web designer if your business plans are being held up by just one area. Or join a forum if you think you need advice in lots of different areas.

And make a list. You might have a big business plan for the bank, or you may have nothing written down at all. Start by jotting down a few ideas about what you need to do to get your business going. Pin this up over your desk, or in the kitchen where you will see it every day. Keep adding tasks as you think of them, and crossing them off as you do them. Use a year planner if it helps to spread the jobs over time. And remember to be realistic: if you are juggling a family or an existing job as well as starting your own business all these tasks will take time.

Best wishes for your business.

Antonia

---

www.themumpreneurguide.co.uk/secretblog
If you want to stay in touch with lots of info and advice for mums in business, visit The Mumpreneur Guide's Secret Blog. This blog is exclusively for you to get up to date tips and advice. I'll answer your questions and share my experiences. If you get stuck on one aspect of business, ask for help. And you can let me know your success stories too.

Family Friendly Working

Are you wondering whether to **return to work** after maternity leave?

Do you feel **torn between work** and spending time with **your children**?

Do you dream of being a **mumpreneur**?

Would you love to find work that **fits in with the family**?

The Family Friendly Working book and **free** Ideas and Inspirations e-course has **the answers you need**

www.familyfriendlyworking.co.uk